ACKNOWLEDGMENTS

I0438709

The U.S. Department of Transportation Volpe National Transportation Systems Center, in coordination with the U.S. Fish and Wildlife Service (USFWS), prepared this study, which was funded by a grant from the Federal Transit Administration Paul S. Sarbanes Transit in Parks Program. The Volpe Center project team included Haley Peckett and David Spiller of the Transportation Planning Division and Scott Lian of the Energy Technology Division.

The authors wish to thank the numerous organizations and individuals who graciously provided their time, knowledge and guidance in the development of this report. Those of particular note are listed below:

Graham Taylor, Refuge Manager (U.S. Fish and Wildlife Service, Parker River National Wildlife Refuge)
Frank Drauszewski, Deputy Refuge Manager (U.S. Fish and Wildlife Service, Parker River National Wildlife Refuge)
Matt Poole, Supervisory Park Ranger (U.S. Fish and Wildlife Service, Parker River National Wildlife Refuge)
Jeff Mast, Regional Roads Coordinator (U.S. Fish and Wildlife Service, Region 5)

Ray Faucher, District Manager (Massachusetts Department of Conservation and Recreation)
Bill Gette (Joppa Flats Education Center, Massachusetts Audubon)
Bill Steelman, Director of Heritage Development (Essex National Heritage Commission)
Michael T. Strauss (City of Newburyport)

CONTENTS

SECTION 1: INTRODUCTION

Parker River National Wildlife Refuge (NWR), located on Plum Island in northeastern Massachusetts, is a major destination for visitors from across New England to observe wildlife within a nationally-significant birding habitat area. Approximately 250,000 visitors come to Parker River NWR annually for a range of Refuge-based activities.

While the Refuge encourages visitation in a manner consistent with the preservation of Parker River's natural resources, the visitors themselves can also bring congestion and conflicts. The Refuge has a mission of protecting species and their habitat, and sensitive areas often dictate the type and location of visitor infrastructure. Also, visitors that come to the Refuge for beach recreation activities exceed the Refuge's capacity for parking during summer months. Refuge staff must carefully balance management activities so that visitors can learn about and enjoy the Refuge's wildlife resources while also ensuring that these resources remain protected.

Specifically, Refuge staff must address several underlying issues:
1. The Refuge experiences parking and road congestion, leading to Refuge closures, on a daily basis during peak visitation periods.
2. Vehicles associated with refuge visitors negatively impact the Refuge's natural resources.
3. Visitors participating in beach-based recreation activities occupy the Refuge's limited parking spaces and may prevent other visitors from participating in wildlife observation, interpretation, or environmental education activities during peak visitation periods.
4. Visitors who participate in interpretation programs, environmental education programs, and special events usually must provide their own transportation and have limited interaction with Refuge staff.

The Refuge is considering the acquisition of a transit vehicle that can address these challenges. The Refuge believes that a transit vehicle could significantly enhance its programmatic offerings and help its partners to decrease vehicle miles traveled (VMT) associated with their programs. Through connecting more visitors to interpretation and environmental education programs with the use of a transit vehicle, Refuge staff believes that they could better accommodate wildlife-oriented visitors during peak periods. A transit vehicle may also reduce congestion on refuge roads and parking lots. A key goal of this report is to explore whether a transit vehicle can address these challenges and meet the Refuge's goals.

Study Background

The Parker River Transit Planning Study stems from several previous analyses and efforts to address multimodal transportation on the Refuge. The study most directly originates from an application that Refuge staff submitted in 2009 to the Federal Transit Administration's (FTA) Paul S. Sarbanes Transit in Parks (TRIP) program. FTA awarded the Refuge $122,300 for the purchase of a transit vehicle. Due to changes in funding needs, U.S. Fish and Wildlife Service (FWS) leadership set aside a portion of the grant funds to complete a transit planning study. The study would define the Refuge's need for a transit vehicle and provide a plan for the purchase, management, and operations of the vehicle.

The Transit Planning Study also builds on the foundation established through several previous transportation-related studies. In 2001, the Federal Highway Administration (FHWA) and FTA worked jointly to complete a series of Field Reports on public land units to assess the transportation system needs and recommend alternative transportation system (ATS) alternatives to address these needs. The Field

Report for Parker River NWR summarized Refuge background and visitation, existing physical conditions, planning and coordination, and feasible transit alternatives. The key recommendations include the purchase of a clean fuel bus for Refuge tours and improved transit service to the Refuge entrance.[1]

In January 2008, the Essex National Heritage Commission (ENHC) sponsored a planning feasibility study to develop a network of non-motorized bicycle and pedestrian routes from the Newburyport commuter rail station to the Parker River NWR and its headquarters. Through the TRIP program, the FTA provided funds to ENHC to complete the feasibility study. The Parker River National Wildlife Refuge Access Project recommended two phases of improvements; the first would improve direct bicycle and pedestrian access along existing roads and the second would create new off-road, multi-use paths to improve connectivity between Newburyport and the Refuge.[2] Since the study's completion, ENHC has worked with sponsors to improve signage and striping and has constructed the first mile of trail network between the commuter rail station and downtown Newburyport.

Finally, the analysis resulting from this Transit Planning Study will inform the Refuge's Comprehensive Conservation Plan (CCP), which the Refuge is completing in association with FWS Region 5 staff between 2011 and 2013. The CCP will guide management decisions on the Refuge over the next 15 years. Refuge and regional staff will incorporate the findings and recommendations from the Transit Planning Study into the Refuge's long-term plans for visitor management, interpretation and environmental education programs, and transportation infrastructure. The Refuge may also consider a more comprehensive and multi-modal transportation study as a next step to both the Transit Planning Study and the CCP.

Goals

Refuge staff have four goals for the potential purchase of a transit vehicle. The goals relate to both existing conditions and challenges on the Refuge, as described in the introduction, as well as to the Refuge's mission. The Refuge's mission includes the following components:

- Provide feeding, resting, and nesting habitat for migratory birds;
- Protect threatened and endangered species; and
- Include wildlife-dependent recreation, where appropriate.[3]

Table 1 lists the four goals of the Transit Feasibility Study along with the evaluation criteria associated with them. The evaluation criteria present quantifiable measures so that the Refuge can estimate the impacts of utilizing a transit vehicle with respect to each goal. The analysis will consider these goals and evaluation criteria in both the overall feasibility of a transit vehicle purchase and in vehicle acquisition and utilization.

---

[1] Federal Highway Administration and Federal Transit Administration. 2001. Field Report – Parker River National Wildlife Refuge. From the Federal Lands Alternative Transportation Systems Study, August 2001. At the time of the report's publication in 2001, the Merrimack Valley Regional Transit Authority and a private trolley company operated transit service from downtown Newburyport to Plum Island.
[2] Vanasse Hangen Brustlin, Inc. 2008. Parker River National Wildlife Refuge Access Project Report. Prepared for the Essex National Heritage Commission.
[3] U.S. Fish and Wildlife Service. 2011. "About Us." *Parker River National Wildlife Refuge – About Us.* Accessed 14 April: http://www.fws.gov/northeast/parkerriver/aboutus.html.

Table 1: Goals and Evaluation Criteria

Goal	Evaluation Criteria
1. Expand visitor opportunities for interpretation and environmental education	• Number of participants in refuge-led environmental education and interpretation programs • Number of environmental education and interpretation programs offered per year • Percentage of environmental education and interpretation programs with a transit option
2. Reduce vehicular congestion on the refuge related to environmental education and interpretive programs 　a. Reduce vehicular impacts to plant and animal species 　b. Increase the safety of visitors and staff 　c. Reduce congestion and enhance visitor experience during festivals and special events	• Estimated VMT associated with environmental education programs • Number (or percentage) of visitors served by transit during special events
3. Demonstrate environmental leadership in transportation related to interpretation and environmental education	• Estimated fuel use associated with environmental education programs • Fuel purchase data for overall refuge activities
4. Engage partners to enhance environmental education opportunities and leverage funding and capacity for vehicle operation and management	• Percentage of vehicle miles traveled to serve partner programs or access partner destinations • Percentage of vehicle operations, maintenance, and/or capital costs shared by partners

Table 1 lists the goals approximately in order of the Refuge's priorities. The Refuge envisions a transit vehicle as primarily serving to expand visitor opportunities for interpretation and environmental education programs. The Refuge also recognizes the importance of congestion management, given the frequency of Refuge closures. Finally, the Refuge values environmental leadership and partnerships, but it recognizes these goals as secondary to the first two goals.

Methods

The purpose of this analysis is to explore the feasibility of a transit vehicle on the Refuge. The project team measured the need for a transit vehicle, assessed the type of vehicle that would be most appropriate, and evaluated when and where the vehicle would be utilized. Section 1 of this report describes the project goals and background. Section 2, Existing Conditions, considers the existing conditions on the Refuge in the context of recognizing challenges and needs related to the use of a transit vehicle. These needs include the areas of visitation, programming and special events, infrastructure and parking, and congestion. The demand analysis in Section 3 examines current and future visitation trends, including participation rates in environmental education and interpretive programs and special events. The project team estimated anticipated future growth in program and event attendance on the basis of visitation patterns in the past several years.

Given the estimate of visitors and route miles of travel that a vehicle would serve, as well as the physical limitations of the Refuge and the capacity of Refuge staff, the project team evaluated several vehicles available for acquisition in Section 4, including consideration of special options, fuel, and maintenance. In Section 5, the project team assessed performed a utilization analysis. Considering the existing physical conditions and visitation patterns, the project team categorized potential uses of a transit vehicle for interpretive and environmental educational programs and special events, as well as a secondary, shuttling function. The team delineated the routes and mileage for each type of use. Then, the team created a mock schedule for one calendar year including all anticipated use activities, including program and event dates and times provided by Refuge staff, refuge partners, and special event websites (listed in Appendix A). The project team then looked for periods of overlapping use and periods of inactivity. During unutilized periods, the project team filled in mandatory uses, such as preventative maintenance, and optional uses that align with the Refuge's priorities, such as transport for school and senior groups. The project team tested the feasibility of scheduling limited, program-focused shuttle service between the Refuge and the Newburyport commuter rail station. In Section 6, the project team also estimated the capital, operations, and maintenance costs of a transit vehicle, as well as potential funding sources (see also Table 22).

Finally, the Transit Planning Study includes an Evaluation Framework and Conclusions component in Section 7, listing evaluation criteria aligned with the study's goals. Section 7 also provides performance targets for the use of a transit vehicle, which can both help the Refuge to plan for the vehicle and to track progress when and if they purchase a vehicle.

SECTION 2: EXISTING CONDITIONS

Refuge Location and Overview

Parker River NWR consists of 4,662 acres on the southern three-fourths of Plum Island, a barrier island in northeastern Massachusetts, 38 miles north of Boston. The Atlantic Ocean borders the east side of the Refuge, and the municipalities of Newbury, Rowley, and Ipswich border the west side. Parker River is considered to be one of the top ten birding destinations in the country and includes the extensive salt marshes between Plum Island and the mainland to the west. The Refuge is of vital significance for waterfowl, shorebirds, and songbirds during pre- and post-breeding migratory periods. More than 300 species of birds, along with a diversity of mammals, reptiles, amphibians, insects and plants thrive in a variety of habitats.[4] FWS constructed a new headquarters, visitor center, and maintenance facility (the Refuge headquarters) in 2003; the facilities are located on 12 acres of land in the City of Newburyport, along the Plum Island Turnpike (the main vehicular access route to the Refuge). The headquarters is also located directly across from the Massachusetts Audubon Society's ("Mass Audubon") Joppa Flats Education Center, which is the launching point for many Audubon-led educational programs that visit the Refuge. Sunset Drive (which becomes Refuge Road within the Refuge) is the sole thoroughfare within the Refuge and provides access to all parking and observation areas for visitor access via a single access point, terminating at Sandy Point State Reservation at the southern tip of Plum Island (see Figure 1).[5]

---

[4] U.S. Fish and Wildlife Service. 2011. Accessed 3 March: http://www.fws.gov/northeast/parkerriver/.
[5] Parker River National Wildlife Refuge Staff (Graham Taylor, Frank Drauszewski, and Matt Poole). 2011. Personal interviews. January 24.

Figure 1 - Parker River National Wildlife Refuge Area Map

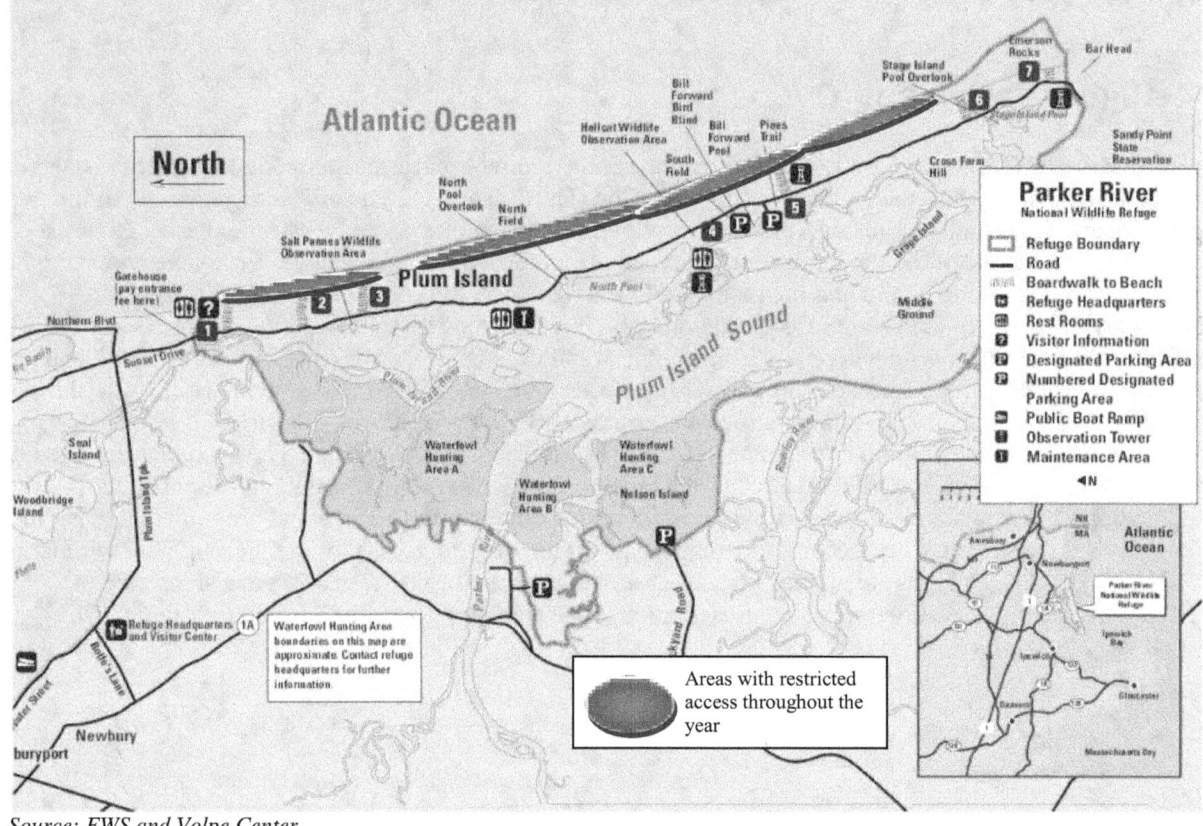

Source: FWS and Volpe Center

The Refuge has several types of habitats and resource areas. The easternmost habitat type is beach and dunes, which are used for nesting, feeding, and resting for piping plovers, least terns, and other shorebirds. The Refuge contains extensive salt marshes, with grasslands, mud flats, and open-water salt pannes, as well as fresh-to-brackish water impoundments and shrub thickets. The salt marshes are home to waterfowl during fall and winter months. The Refuge's maritime forests, located on Plum Island between the dunes and the Plum Island Sound, house songbirds such as warblers, kestrels, and woodcock, during the spring and fall months. Hawks, eagles, and owls also come to the Refuge's forests and shrub lands during the winter.[6]

While the Refuge is a destination for beachgoers, birders, hunters and anglers, the Refuge staff's primary responsibility is to preserve and protect the habitats and wildlife within its boundary. In support of this mission, which places "Wildlife First," the Refuge restricts visitor access to its beaches from April 1 through early summer. Maintaining access restrictions while simultaneously managing high visitation in the spring and summer months is a challenge for the Refuge staff.

---

[6] U.S. Fish and Wildlife Service. 2011. Accessed 3 March: http://www.fws.gov/northeast/parkerriver/wildlife.html.

Seasonality

Parker River NWR's natural resource management, visitor management, programs, special events, and travel patterns are all highly dependent upon a seasonal calendar. The migration of birds and other wildlife dictates the areas of the Refuge that can be open to visitor access. Climate, school calendars, and community events affect visitation levels and types of activities. Recognizing the key role of seasons in the management of the Refuge and the utilization of a transit vehicle, Table 2 provides an overview of the interplay between seasonal visitation, wildlife management, and climate. Throughout the Existing Conditions section, seasonal descriptions document how conditions vary during the year.

Visitation also follows seasonal trends. The Refuge received between 240,000 and 290,000 visitors each year between 2008 and 2010. Visitation levels were between 30,000 and 50,000 per month between June and September, with most visitors coming for beach recreation. Visitation levels dropped to 10,000 visitors or fewer per month in December and January. Visitation by school groups is concentrated in the spring and fall. The report describes visitation in greater detail later in this section.

Table 2 - Seasonal Visitation & Events

Month	Jan	Feb	Mar	Apr	May	Jun	Jul	Aug	Sep	Oct	Nov	Dec
Monthly Visitation	8,626	11,316	15,804	19,809	27,616	23,479	35,452	44,050	35,898	17,222	11,775	9,043
Educational Programs	8	8	8	9	9	16	13	10	10	9	9	8
Special Events		• Eagle Festival • Snowy Owl Program • Nature Photography Workshop	Beach Clean-Up			• Go Fish • Open House at Great Bay NWR	• Gulf of Maine Institute Annual Conference • Digital Nature Photography Camp • Riverfront Music Festival • Yankee Homecoming	Yankee Home-coming	• Open House at Great Bay NWR • Beach Clean-Up • Trails & Sails	• National Wildlife Refuge Week Activities		
Seasonal Closures	Refuge road may close due to snow / ice, particularly beyond Hellcat Observation Area where the road is unpaved			Beach Closed (Lots 2, 3, 6 and 7) for piping plover nesting season			Partial beach closures (Lots 2, 3, 6 and 7)				Closed for occasional hunting events; Refuge road may close due to snow / ice	

Information based on data provided by Refuge staff. See individual sections for data citations.

Transportation Infrastructure

The physical and transportation infrastructure allows for the management of natural resources, visitor access, and the provision of education and interpretive programs and special events. The vehicles, roads, parking lots, and buildings within the Refuge affect both the management activities of staff and the ways that visitors take advantage of refuge resources. The physical and transportation infrastructure present opportunities and constraints that will help determine the type of transit vehicle that would most effectively address Refuge needs.

Vehicle Fleet

Parker River NWR currently owns 14 vehicles, which are stored in an uncovered parking lot at the Refuge headquarters. The Refuge owns maintenance vehicles, including two heavy-duty pickup trucks, SUVs, and passenger cars, along with several pieces of heavy equipment. The current fleet includes a ten-passenger van and a seven-passenger minivan that are occasionally used to transport visitors and support small group tours. An inventory of the Refuge's vehicle fleet is listed in Table 3.

Table 3 - Parker River NWR Vehicle Fleet

Vehicle Description	Purpose	Quantity	General Staff Use	Use for Visitor Transport	Fuel Type
10-passenger van	Staff use, group programs	1	Yes	Yes	Gasoline
7-passenger Chevy Uplander	Staff use, group programs	1	Yes	Yes	Gasoline
Ford Escape SUV	Staff use	1	Yes	No	Gasoline
Chevy Silverado pick-up truck	Staff use	1	Yes	No	Gasoline
Chevy Malibu sedan	Staff use	1	Yes	No	Gasoline
Chevy HHR	Staff use	1	Yes	No	Gasoline
Dodge pick-up truck	Staff use	1	Yes	No	Gasoline
Dodge Dakota	Staff use	1	Yes	No	Gasoline
Law enforcement vehicles	Law enforcement	3	No	No	Gasoline
Dual-wheel pick-up truck	Maintenance, plowing	2	No	No	Diesel
Dump truck	Material hauling	1	No	No	Diesel

Source: Refuge staff

If the passenger vans are available, Refuge staff will use these vehicles for group tours on the Refuge. However, the passenger vans are often in use by the Youth Conservation Corps programs and staff management activities, especially during summer months. The Refuge also rents vehicles from Salter Transportation Inc. for some Refuge programs and special events, which are described in later sections.

The Refuge does not own any vehicles that can accommodate more than 10 passengers or that could be dedicated to program use. The Refuge does have the capability to operate and maintain a range of vehicle types.

Fueling and Maintenance

The Refuge staff fuel their vehicles at the maintenance facility located at the Refuge headquarters, utilizing two above-ground 500 gallon capacity ConVault fuel tanks (gasoline and diesel). Staff also use purchase cards to fuel vehicles at local gas stations as needed. The Refuge uses commercial gasoline (standard 10 percent ethanol content) and ultra-low sulfur diesel (ULSD) for its vehicle fleet. The Refuge has shown an interest in biodiesel, but staff have not tried using biodiesel due to concerns about its performance in the diesel-powered heavy equipment and its viscosity at cold temperatures. The Refuge may test the use of biodiesel by using a low blend such as B5 (consisting of 95 percent ULSD with a 5 percent biodiesel blend) during the colder months and switching to a standard blend of B20 (80 percent ULSD, 20 percent biodiesel) during the warmer months.[7]

The total fuel tank capacity at the Refuge currently is 1,000 gallons. Facilities with more than 1,320 gallons of above-ground storage of oil or oil products are subject to the U.S. Environmental Protection Agency's Spill Prevention Control and Countermeasure (SPCC) regulation (40 CFR Part 112).[8]

Figure 2 - Parker River Vehicle Fueling

Source: Volpe Center

The Refuge headquarters also has an onsite maintenance garage with service bays. The garage includes a hydraulic vehicle lift and tools suitable for minor repairs, oil changes, and general maintenance. The garage can accommodate passenger vehicles, vans, and large pickup trucks. The depth of the garage bay (22 feet) limits the length of vehicles that can fit inside; the garage is sufficiently wide (12-14 feet) and tall to accommodate most vehicles. The garage may be able to accommodate a small shuttle bus, depending upon the length of the bus. Refuge staff bring vehicles to several local repair facilities for maintenance needs that the Refuge cannot accommodate at its headquarters.

---

[7] Parker River National Wildlife Refuge Staff. 2011.
[8] U.S. Environmental Protection Agency. 2011. Spill Prevention, Control, and Countermeasure Rule. *SPCC Rule – Emergency Management – US EPA*. Accessed 3 March: http://www.epa.gov/ceppo/web/content/spcc/.

Figure 3 - Parker River Vehicle Maintenance Garage

Source: Volpe Center

The existing fueling infrastructure is of sufficient capacity to accommodate on-site fueling of a shuttle bus. The Refuge could accommodate a vehicle that uses gasoline, diesel, or biodiesel. The Refuge also has capabilities to manage basic maintenance for a transit vehicle, although the garage would not be able to accommodate transit vehicles over 22 feet long. Considering the Refuge's capacity to store and maintain other large vehicles, the Refuge could also feasibly maintain a larger vehicle and rely on off-site service as needed.

Surrounding Amenities and Transportation Facilities

In addition to the Refuge lands and associated facilities, several surrounding destinations impact travel patterns associated with Refuge visitation:

- A Massachusetts Bay Transportation Authority (MBTA) commuter rail station in Newburyport is located approximately 4.5 miles from the Refuge entrance and 1.8 miles from the Refuge headquarters (see Figure 4). MBTA offers commuter rail service to Boston's North Station and other towns along the North Shore. MBTA runs 13 round trips on weekdays and six round trips on weekends.[9]
- The C&J bus company owns a park and ride lot located in Newburyport at the northeast quadrant of the Interstate 95 interchange with Route 113. C&J offers bus service to Boston's South Station and Logan Airport. C&J runs approximately 30 round-trip buses each weekday and approximately 20 round-trip buses on weekends and holidays. The C&J park and ride lot is located 4.3 miles from the Refuge Headquarters.[10]

---

[9] Massachusetts Bay Transportation Authority. 2010. Newbury/Rockport Line. Accessed 13 January 2011: http://www.mbta.com/schedules_and_maps/rail/.
[10] C&J. 2009. NH Seacoast/Newburyport, MA to Logan Airport & Downtown Boston. Accessed 13 January 2011: http://www.ridecj.com.

Figure 4 – Bus & MBTA Commuter Rail Station Proximity

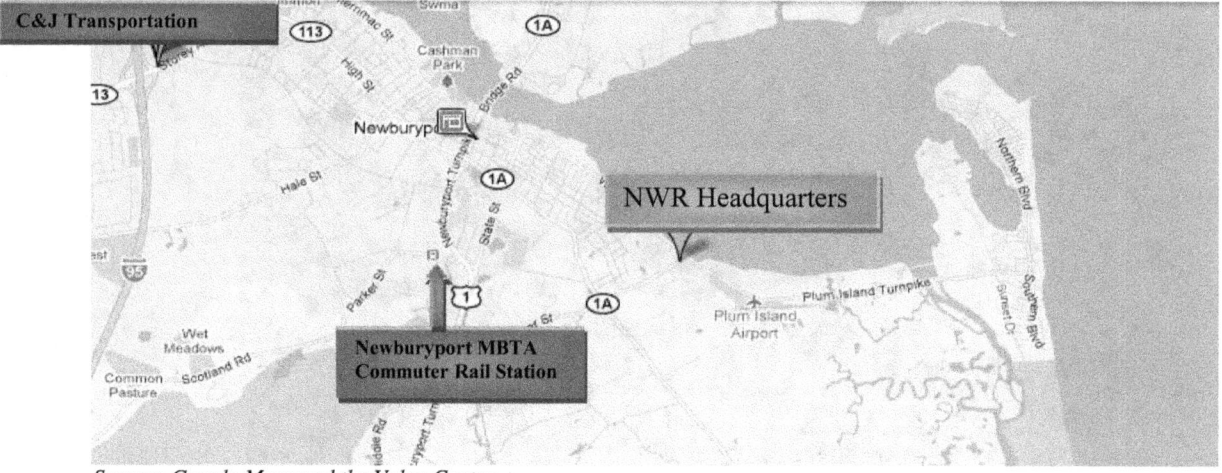

Source: Google Maps and the Volpe Center

- The Mass Audubon's Joppa Flats Education Center is located across the Plum Island Turnpike from the Parker River NWR Visitor Center. The facility, which was planned in conjunction with the Refuge headquarters, opened in 2003. Mass Audubon uses the Refuge as a primary site for its environmental education programs. Approximately 277 Mass Audubon educational programs bring visitors to the Refuge each year.[11]
- Sandy Point Reservation is a 77-acre beachfront park located at the southern end of Plum Island, with all vehicular access channeled through the Refuge entrance and along Refuge Road. The Massachusetts Department of Conservation and Recreation (DCR) owns and manages Sandy Point, although the Refuge has the right to restrict vehicular access when the parking lot is full. Sandy Point is very popular with beachgoers and fills quickly during summer months.[12]

Refuge Road & Parking Overview

Refuge Road (which is named Sunset Drive north of the Refuge entrance gate) is the sole thoroughfare through the Refuge and terminates at Sandy Point Beach and Reservation at the southern tip of Plum Island. The 6.54-mile Refuge Road is paved for the northernmost 3.65 miles, with a gravel and crushed aggregate surface for the southern 2.89 miles. The road is the only vehicular and non-motorized access route to most Refuge facilities, trails, parking lots 1 through 7, wildlife overlooks, observation towers, and interpretive displays (see Figure 5). Refuge Road has a speed limit of 25 miles per hour, and is open to passenger vehicles, buses and vans, bicyclists, and pedestrians.

---

[11] Gette, Bill. 2011. Personal interview. January 24 and February 18.
[12] Massachusetts DCR. 2011. Sandy Point State Reservation. Accessed 3 March: http://www.mass.gov/dcr/parks/northeast/sndp.htm; and Faucher, Ray. 2011. Personal interview. January 19.

Figure 5 - Map of Refuge Road

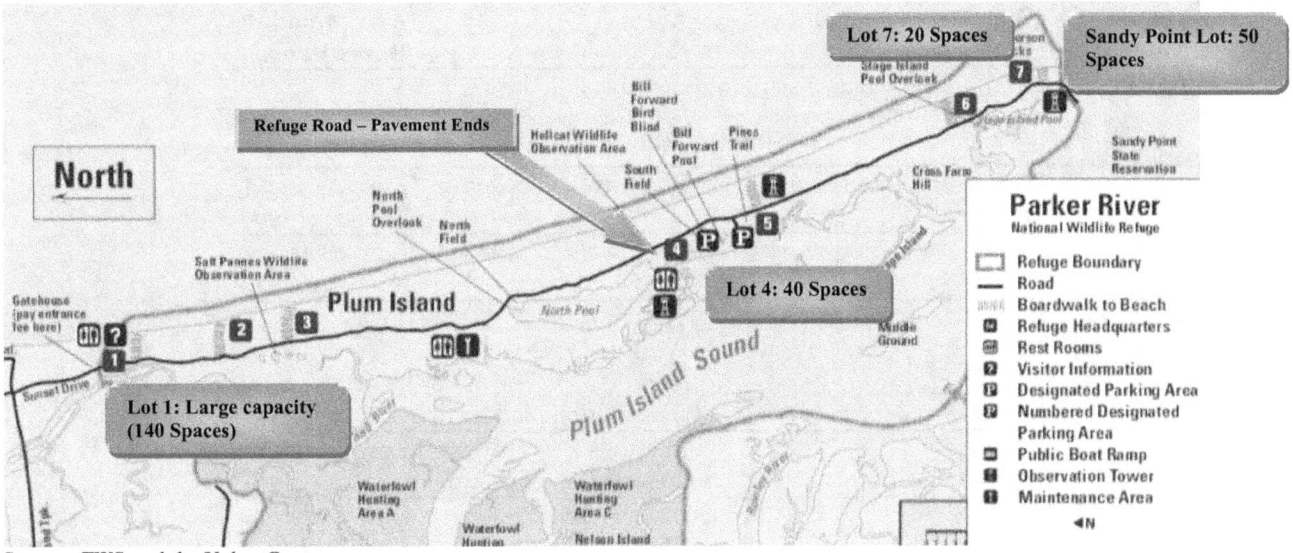

Source: FWS and the Volpe Center

The Refuge contains nine parking lots, seven of which are located on Plum Island. The remaining two are located in Rowley and offer access to the waterfowl hunting areas (tan shaded in Fig. 5 above); these lots are not within the scope of the transit analysis. The description and capacity of lots 1 through 7 can be found in Table 4 (below) and are detailed in the following section. Congestion often occurs at popular wildlife observation areas alongside the North Pool and adjacent to lots 2 through 7. Visitors often pull over or park in these areas, even during periods of lot closures or restrictions.[13]

---

[13] Parker River National Wildlife Refuge Staff. 2011.

Table 4 – Parker NWR Parking Lots on Plum Island

Lot Number	Vehicle Capacity	Amenities	Access	Accommodates Buses/Vans
1	140	Contact station Restrooms	Boardwalk to beach Wildlife observation area	Yes
2	32	Interpretive display	Boardwalk to beach	Low visitation periods only
3	33	Interpretive display	Boardwalk to beach	Low visitation periods only
4	40	Restrooms, Trail	Trail to Hellcat Wildlife Observation Area Observation platform	Yes
5	8		Boardwalk to beach Observation platform	Low visitation periods only
6	25		Boardwalk to beach Wildlife overlook	Low visitation periods only
7	20		Boardwalk to beach Observation platform	Low visitation periods only
Pines Trail	10-12	Trail	Trail access	Vans only
Bill Forward Observation Blind	6	Trail to observation blind	Bird blind; wildlife observation area	Vans only
Sub-HQ	6	Restrooms, access to clam flats	Access for staff vehicles; maintenance equipment storage	Vans only
North Pool Overlook	5	Observation area	Wildlife observation area	Vans only

In general, the only lots that can easily accommodate buses and allow for their turnaround are lots 1 and 4. Other lots can accommodate bus maneuvers during low visitation periods when there are fewer cars parked there, but the Refuge has experienced issues in the past with buses that could not sufficiently turn around on the southern portion of the Refuge during high visitation days (due to heavy traffic in parking lots and on the Refuge Road).

Lot 1 – 140 Spaces
Located immediately within the entrance gates along Refuge Road, lot 1 is the highest-capacity parking area within the Refuge and can hold approximately 140 cars. This lot provides direct access to the beach via a boardwalk and path located at the eastern end of the lot and extending to the beach. It also offers access to wildlife observation areas, both east and west of Refuge Road. Lot 1 remains open year-round, including when the rest of the Refuge beach is closed from April 1st through June. Lot 1 is also the location of the visitor contact station and restroom s facilities.

Figure 6 - Lot 1

Source: Google Maps and the Volpe Center

Lot 2 (32 Spaces) and Lot 3 (33 Spaces)
Located on the eastern side of Refuge Road approximately 2,500 feet south of lot 1, lots 2 and 3 are medium-capacity lots with 32 and 33 spaces, respectively. They both have similar layouts with parking spaces arranged in one row perpendicular to Refuge Road. Both lots provide access to boardwalks that lead visitors to the beach. Additionally, these areas offer some wildlife viewing locations. They are closed throughout piping plover season from April through August.

Lot 4(40 Spaces)
Lot 4 is located midway between the gatehouse entrance and Sandy Point, near the Hellcat Wildlife Observation area. The Hellcat area includes restrooms, a trail, and an observation platform. Beyond this lot, the Refuge Road is an unpaved, gravel road. Lot 4 can accommodate buses and remains open throughout the year. Beach closures do not affect lot 4 because it does not provide pedestrian access to the beach.

Figure 7 – Lot 2

Source: Google Maps

19

Figure 8 - Lot 4

Source: Google Maps

Lots 5 (8 Spaces) and 6 (25 Spaces)
Lots 5 and 6 are situated along the roadside, with layouts similar to those of lots 2 and 3. Lot 5 provides access to an observation platform and remains open year-round. Lot 6 provides 25 parking spaces for visitor access to the beach. Lot 6 is usually closed for all or most of the plover season as it provides direct access to the beach via a walking path.

Figure 9 – Lots 5 and 6

Source: Google Maps

Lot 7 (20 Spaces)
Lot 7 is located just north of the southern Refuge boundary, adjacent to Sandy Point Reservation. Lot 7 has limited parking (20 spaces) and provides access to Emerson Rocks and the Stage Island Pool, which are vantage points for wildlife observation. Lot 6 is usually closed for part of the plover season.

Figure 10 - Lot 7

Source: Google Maps

Sandy Point Lots
The two parking lots at Sandy Point have a total capacity of 50 cars. The lots offer access to the beaches and trails of Sandy Point Reservation. This lot is usually the first to reach capacity during the summer beach recreation season, followed by Lot 1. Once the Sandy Point lot reaches capacity, which can happen several times per day during the summer months, DCR staff, when available, notify Refuge staff at the gatehouse, who then restrict access for Sandy Point. During times when DCR staff are not present at Sandy Point, the Refuge staff will periodically check Sandy Point lots by vehicle, as capacity allows.

Figure 11 – Upper and Lower Sandy Point Lot

Source: Google Maps

Seasonality and Parking

The Refuge closes most of the parking lots during several months of the year due to species presence or weather conditions. The piping plover is a federally protected threatened species and nests along the beaches. Also closed are many of the parking lots offering beach access beginning in April and ending in August (although lot 1 remains open year-round). Table 1 shows seasonal parking lot closures due to piping plovers. During plover season, the refuge staff greatly reduces total parking availability on Plum Island due to beach access lot closures, but other lots for wildlife observation remain open. Lots that remain open during piping plover season include lot 4 (40 spaces), lot 5 (eight spaces), an eight-space lot by the Pines trail (near South Hellcat), a six-car lot near the North Pool, a lot by the sub-headquarters building near the maintenance facility and restrooms (six to eight cars), and a live parking lot on the west side of Refuge Road near the salt pannes (visitors using the live parking lot may not leave their vehicles unattended). Additionally, the Refuge opens several spots at lots 6 and 7 for wildlife observation activities during piping plover season.

While the Refuge maintains and plows the Refuge Road, the Road may be closed to visitors due to extreme weather conditions. Staff occasionally closes the Road south of lot 4 for one to three weeks during major snow storms or flooding events. All parking lots south of lot 4 also close during these periods.

The Sandy Point parking lots are extremely popular during summer months. FWS and DCR staff report that visitors travel at high speeds on the Refuge road early on summer mornings to claim one of the 50 parking spaces at Sandy Point. Staff also report that some Sandy Point visitors will park at the non-beach-access lots on the Refuge and walk or bike the remaining distance to Sandy Point. DCR only keeps the upper lot of Sandy Point open during winter months.

Traffic Analysis

Visitors accessing Parker River NWR via land-based transportation modes must travel on the Plum Island Turnpike to Sunset Drive, which becomes Refuge Road (refer to Figure 1). (Visitors whose trips originate on Plum Island do not need to use Plum Island Turnpike). The Merrimack Valley Planning Commission (MVPC) recorded Average Daily Traffic (ADT) of 10,530 in August 2009 on the Plum Island Turnpike. The ADT was down from 12,061 vehicles in July 2004.[14] Massachusetts Department of Transportation (MassDOT) recorded ADT of 7,500 on the bridge of Plum Island Turnpike in 2004, although MassDOT does not include data on the month of the traffic count.[15] In both cases, not all of these vehicles represent Refuge visitors, as many other vehicles access homes, business, or non-Refuge-owned beach facilities on Plum Island. (The Island's residential population swells to 5,000 in the summer months). The Refuge vehicle counts (as listed in Table 5) exceed the MVPC and MassDOT traffic counts, which may be due to repeat daily visitation, staff travel throughout the Refuge, or discrepancies in counting methodology between MVPC and the Refuge.[16]

Refuge Road provides access to many wildlife observation areas and Refuge amenities and is the only land-based access to the Sandy Point Reservation. The Refuge controls access to Refuge Road, and to most visitation areas of the Refuge, through a gatehouse located at the northern Refuge boundary. All

---

[14] Merrimack Valley Planning Commission. 2010. MVPC History of Average Daily Traffic (1999-2009). Accessed 13 January 2011: http://www.mvpc.org/index.asp?menu=wp128200612324&page=wp1292006162129.

[15] MassDOT. 2011. Traffic Counts for Newbury. Accessed 3 March: http://www.mhd.state.ma.us/traffic.asp?f=1&C=NEWBURY. Note that MassDOT does not provide a capacity analysis or level of service for Plum Island Turnpike.

16 Note that the traffic counts of 22,500 and 20,563 in August of 2009 and 2010, respectively, appear to be far above normal monthly traffic on the Refuge. These rare events may be part of the reason for differences between Refuge data and MVPC data.

vehicles must pass through the gatehouse and pay a Refuge entrance fee. Bicyclists and pedestrians must also pay an entrance fee at the gatehouse. The Refuge maintains a traffic counter at the gatehouse that records all vehicles that enter the Refuge. Table 5 details vehicle counts by month for years 2007-2011. Due to a malfunctioning traffic counter from 2005 through 2007, the Refuge only has traffic data from 2007 through the first months of Fiscal Year 2011.[17]

Table 5: Monthly Vehicle Counts at Gatehouse

Fiscal Year	2007 Monthly Vehicles	2008 Monthly Vehicles	2009 Monthly Vehicles	2010 Monthly Vehicles	2011 Monthly Vehicles	Avg. Visitation (2.4 persons per vehicle)
October	7,000	9,313	6,020	5,861	7,685	**17,222**
November	4,728	5,162	6,100	4,525	4,016	**11,775**
December	3,284	3,144	6,135	4,319	1,957	**9,043**
January		5,030	976	4,776		**8,626**
February		4,446	5,000	4,699		**11,316**
March		7,744	7,316	4,695		**15,804**
April		3,844	13,356	7,561		**19,809**
May		10,363	11,214	12,943		**27,616**
June		12,984	9,300	7,065		**23,479**
July		14,677	16,259	13,379		**35,452**
August		12,000	22,500	20,563		**44,050**
September		14,168	15,589	15,116		**35,898**
Total Vehicles	**15,012**	**102,875**	**119,765**	**105,502**	**6,558**	

Source: Parker River NWR traffic counters

The traffic counter recorded over 100,000 vehicles entering the Refuge annually from 2008 through 2010. Table 5 data show several trends across recent years and across seasons. For example, the data show a clear peak in vehicle traffic between May and September, with up to 22,500 vehicles entering the Refuge during the month of August. Although the heaviest traffic is associated with beach recreation, the Refuge experiences consistently high traffic during May and June, when beach access is closed. There are only a few months per year with very low traffic on the Refuge: the number of monthly vehicles driving on the Refuge ranges from 1,000 or fewer to approximately 9,000 during the fall and winter.

During very high visitation months, the Refuge staff will close the Refuge and stagger vehicle entries as parking lots reach capacity. These closures may occur multiple times each day, lasting up to several hours during the busiest periods. The Sandy Point lot reaches capacity quickly on summer mornings. Lot 1, the highest capacity parking lot in the Refuge, is open year-round to accommodate the beach visitation demands. Bicyclists and pedestrians may still enter the Refuge during closure events.[18]

The traffic analysis demonstrates consistent and heavy vehicle traffic during 10 months of the year, with very high traffic during three months of the year. The Refuge infrastructure and staff must accommodate high traffic from May through September, while still maintaining functional capacity for visitation during

---

[17] The Refuge is in the process of adding several new traffic counters in public areas within the Refuge. The additional counters will result in a more detailed understanding of total visitation, along with patterns of visitation within Refuge boundaries.
[18] Parker River National Wildlife Refuge Staff. 2011.

fall and winter months. Later sections of this report describe natural resource and visitor management issues related to heavy traffic.

Partners and Programs

In addition to the physical and transportation infrastructure described in the previous section, the Refuge has established formal and informal programs and partnerships that present needs and opportunities for visitor access and education. The primary goal for a transit vehicle at Parker River NWR is to serve visitors during educational and interpretive programs and special events, often with the assistance of Refuge partners. These partnerships, programs, and special events determine the demand for a transit vehicle.

Visitation Analysis

Parker River NWR is a regional destination Refuge, attracting day trip visitors from across the region. Approximately 253,200 visitors came to Parker River in 2010 and 287,400 visitors came in 2009. Refuge staff estimates that the average annual visitation since 2005 is 248,000, although the Refuge does not have data from 2005 through 2007 due to a malfunctioning traffic counter. The Refuge calculates visitation by multiplying the number of vehicles that pass through the entry gate by an average vehicle occupancy of 2.4 persons per vehicle.[19] Monthly visitation for FY 2007 through 2011 is listed in Table 6.

Table 6: Monthly Visitation Analysis

Fiscal Year	2007	2008	2009	2010	2011
October	16,800	22,351	14,448	14,066	18,444
November	11,347	12,389	14,640	10,860	9,638
December	7,882	7,546	14,724	10,366	4,697
January		12,072	2,342	11,462	
February		10,670	12,000	11,278	
March		18,586	17,558	11,268	
April		9,226	32,054	18,146	
May		24,871	26,914	31,063	
June		31,162	22,320	16,956	
July		35,225	39,022	32,110	
August		28,800	54,000	49,351	
September		34,003	37,414	36,278	
Number of Visitors	**36,028**	**246,900**	**287,436**	**253,204**	**15,739**

Source: Parker River NWR traffic counters

---

[19] The average vehicle occupancy is based upon a visitor use study from the University of New Hampshire, completed in 1995. Parker River National Wildlife Refuge Staff. 2011.

Figure 12: Average Monthly Visitation

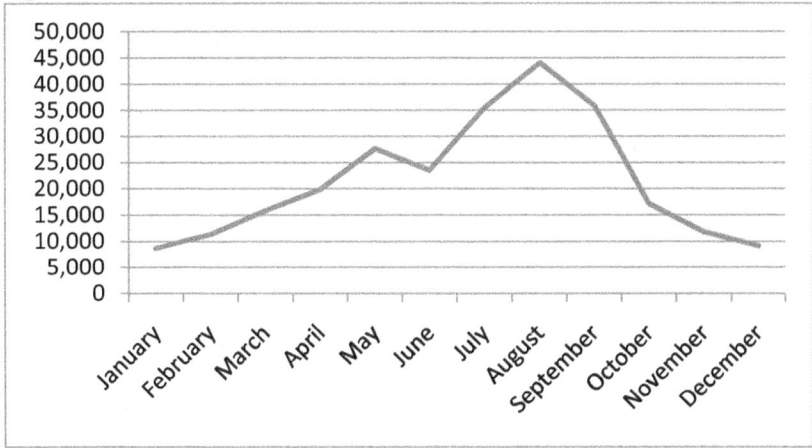

Source: Parker River NWR traffic counters. Data from FY2007 and FY2011 are from October through December only.

Visitors to Parker River participate in wildlife observation, photography, walking, birding, beach recreation, fishing, clamming, hunting, and kayaking. The Refuge Annual Performance Plan (RAPP) uses estimates from Visitor Services staff to calculate approximate visitor participation in specified activities. These numbers list the number of *visits* per year, whereas the monthly visitation listed above lists *visitors*. For example, Refuge staff may count a single visitor multiple times if that visitor participates in several activities over the course of his or her trip to the Refuge and/or visits the Refuge multiple times each year. Therefore, the total number of activity-based visits listed in Table 7 is greater than the number of visitors calculated in Table 6.

Table 7: Refuge Visitation by Activity

Measure	2006	2007	2008	2009	2010
Number of Special Events hosted on- and off-site	6	6	6	6	6
Number of participants in special events on site	1,289	1,011	2,737	3,541	3,500
Visitors to Visitor Center or Contact Station	3,560	3,585	12,814	14,666	13,500
Number of Foot Trail/Pedestrian visits	185,000	191,250	183,618	191,126	209,000
Number of Auto Tour visits	222,750	229,500	220,341	229,351	250,000
Number of Boat Trail/Launch visits	474	474	459	459	540
Total Wildlife Observation visits	408,224	421,224	404,418	446,419	487,405
Number of Photography participants	16,000	63,750	61,206	63,709	69,500
Number of education participants involved in on- and off-site environmental education programs.	5,080	3,971	4,369	5,354	5,350
Number of interpretation participants in on- and off-site talks/programs	3,455	3,639	3,374	6,333	5,324
Total other recreational participants	37,125	153,000	146,894	127,667	133,951

Source: RAPP 2011[20]

---

[20] U.S. Fish and Wildlife Service. 2011. Refuge Annual Performance Plan—Multi-year Measures (Parker River NWR). Provided by Refuge staff 18 February.

As shown in Table 7, the number of visitors to the Refuge for all categories of activities has grown over the past five years. Most notably, the number of Auto Tour visits, or visitors who use their private vehicles to reach Refuge amenities, jumped to 250,000 in 2010, up from 220,000 to 230,000 for the previous four years. The increase in Auto Tour visits may signal a growing need to better manage traffic volume and patterns on Refuge roads.

The Refuge tracked 13,500 visitors to its Visitor Center and the Visitor Contact Station (located on the Refuge adjacent to Lot 1). RAPP data also shows that recreational participants consistently comprise a high proportion of total Refuge visitors. The number of recreational participants provides a challenge for Refuge management to ensure that visitors who come to enjoy the Refuge's natural resources have the opportunity to do so.

The RAPP data also shows noteworthy trends related to programs and special

Seasonality and Visitation

Refuge visitors come to see the many species of birds that utilize the Refuge, with peak birding season occurring from April through June and again from September through October. Environmental education programs and field trips often coincide with these peak seasons.

Approximately 44 percent of the Refuge's total annual visitation occurs between July and September, as thousands of recreational beach visitors join visitors who participate in wildlife-based activities. The Refuge's highest visitation season overlaps with the presence of piping plovers on Plum Island from April through June, during which time the Refuge staff closes beach access. Therefore, visitation for beach recreation activities peaks after plover season. During plover season, the Refuge and its partners run programs (see descriptions in the following section) to offer guided access to the migrating birds.

events. RAPP estimates show that the number of participants in environmental education programs has remained fairly steady, fluctuating between approximately 4,000 and 5,500 participants per year. The Refuge would like to expand this number in the future and improve the quality of programs through the use of a transit vehicle. Interpretive programs participants have increased since 2008, ranging from 3,300 to 6,300 participants per year, demonstrating both the Refuge's initial efforts to make these programs more robust and a growing demand for high-quality interpretive programs. The RAPP data for both environmental education and interpretation program participants combines to an approximate annual total of 10,600. Finally, the number of participants in Refuge special events in 2009 and 2010 has nearly tripled since 2007 and 2008, also signaling increased interest in wildlife-based programming.

Figure 13 – Visitors to the Parker River NWR Visitor Center

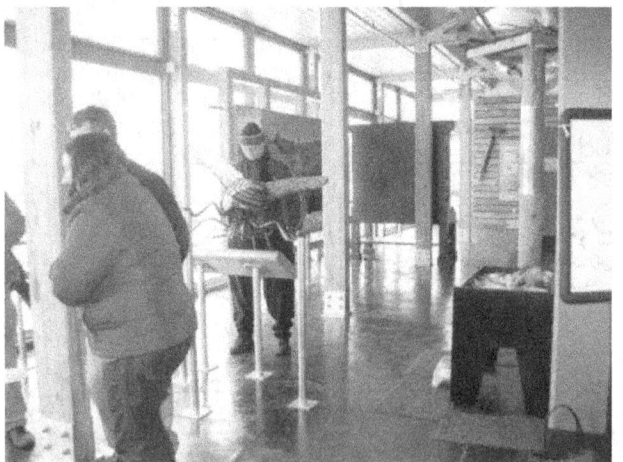

Source: Volpe Center

The Refuge has not formally surveyed visitors for demographic, origin, or trip purpose information since 1995, when the University of New Hampshire conducted an economic study. Anecdotally, Refuge staff note that visitors come from throughout eastern Massachusetts and southern New Hampshire and Maine, with some traveling up to two hours each way to visit the Refuge. Visitors include families with children, retirees, and senior citizens.[21] Refuge staff have actively worked to bring in children through many of its existing environmental education programs. The close partnership with Mass Audubon's Joppa Flats Education Center also draws many children and senior citizens to

---

[21] Federal Highway Administration and Federal Transit Administration. 2001. Field Report – Parker River National Wildlife Refuge.

participate in regular birding programs.[22] The following section provides more information about the programs of the Refuge and its partners.

Refuge Educational and Interpretive Programs

Parker River NWR staff offer year-round educational and interpretive programs to help visitors learn about the unique birds that migrate through the Refuge. Most programs are open to the public, while some programs cater to specific audiences, such as local schools. Programs may be trail-based, with Refuge staff leading walks along boardwalks, or vehicle-based with stops for interpretation (particularly during winter months).

Programs originate at the Refuge headquarters and travel through several points of the Refuge. The Refuge's ten- and seven-passenger vans are sometimes available for Refuge programs. In most cases, the vans cannot fit all program participants or the vans are unavailable for program use, in which case participants use their own vehicles (including school buses for field trips) or the Refuge may rent vehicles for some events and programs. Refuge staff plan program routes based on season, traffic, presence of species, and location of pull-offs where carpooling vehicles can park. Participants that carpool for Refuge programs cannot communicate with Refuge staff for questions or information, except during designated stops.[23] Most programs follow routes that range from 12 to 16 miles round-trip from the Refuge headquarters. Programs that rely upon private vehicles may include up to eight vehicles, with a range of 24 to 128 VMT per program. The Refuge has historically run approximately four programs per month, with an increase in frequency from May through October.[24]

Figure 14 – Eagle Watching along the Merrimack River

Source: Volpe Center

The Refuge has traditionally focused its environmental education programs on children, including field trips for school groups, summer day camp programs, and early childhood education workshops. For example, the Refuge has an ongoing partnership with Newburyport High School and the Gulf of Maine Institute in which local high school students visit the Refuge each month to learn about and manage invasive species. Refuge staff also lead interpretive programs for adults and families to view seasonal birds on the Refuge. Typically, the schools and other groups that participate in Refuge education and interpretive programs originate from the Merrimack River area. Refuge staff would like to expand their audience to the cities of Lawrence and Lowell, which are located 20 to 30 miles west of the Refuge and contain populations that are typically underserved by the Refuge.[25]

---

[22] Parker River National Wildlife Refuge Staff. 2011.
[23] Ibid.
[24] Poole, Matt. 2011. Predicted Bus Use at Parker River National Wildlife Refuge. (Provided to the Volpe Center by the Refuge staff).
[25] Parker River National Wildlife Refuge Staff. 2011.

Finally, Parker River staff also manage three additional National Wildlife Refuges in Massachusetts and New Hampshire: Great Bay NWR, Thacher Island NWR, and Wapack NWR. Staff occasionally runs programs and field trips to these refuges, for which a transit vehicle may be useful.

Mass Audubon Educational and Interpretive Programs

The Mass Joppa Flats Education Center runs approximately 475 programs per year, of which approximately 277 bring visitors to the Refuge. The programs have a dual purpose: to instill a conservation ethic in participants and to collect program fees that help sustain Mass Audubon's sanctuary and conservation activities. Mass Audubon pays for annual special use permits that allow them to hold programs on the Refuge, and program participants do not have to pay separate entrance fees for the Refuge (beyond the Mass Audubon program fee). Mass Audubon has programs that cater to children, families, and adults, as well as programs that serve special needs groups. During 2010, a total of 5,317 visitors participated in 277 Mass Audubon-led programs at the Refuge.[26] Table 8 shows Mass Audubon program data.

Table 8: Mass Audubon Programs at Parker River NWR

Visitors to the Refuge	
Group program visitors to the Refuge	3,420 (2009) 3,591 (2010)
Group program visitors who used their own buses	2,565 (2009) 2,693 (2010)
Public program visitors to the Refuge	1,623 (2009) 1,726 (2010)
Programs and events on the Refuge	
Public programs that use the Refuge (2010)	190
Group programs that use the Refuge (2010)	87
Wednesday morning birding on the Refuge*	30
Saturday morning birding on the Refuge*	30
Friday morning birding on the Refuge*	4
Wednesday evening birding on the Refuge*	6
Special events on Refuge	1
Average program size	
Average group size of public programs	9
Average group size of weekly birding programs**	25
Average group size of group programs	41

*No registration required
**These include Wednesday, Friday, and Saturday morning birding and Wednesday evening birding
Source: Mass Audubon

For Table 8, group program visitors are defined as the number of visitors who register and participate in Mass Audubon programs as part of a group, including school field trips and retirement communities. Individual visitors are those who register or participate as individuals; this number includes the Wednesday and Saturday morning birding programs. Public programs do not include group programs.

---

[26] Gette, Bill. 2011.

Figure 15 – Educational Programs at Joppa Flats

Source: Volpe Center

The Mass Audubon program data shows that program participation has increased slightly between 2009 and 2010, and staff expects those trends to continue in coming years. The Joppa Flats Education Center runs a total of 379 programs open to the general public, 94 group programs, 10 teacher workshops, and eight special events. Many of these have some program component that takes visitors to the Refuge, as displayed in Table 8. For the 190 public programs that use the Refuge, participants use their own private vehicles or carpool using the three seven-passenger Mass Audubon vans. Approximately 75 percent of group programs, which includes school groups and retirement center groups, use their own buses or vans to transport visitors to the Refuge. The remaining 25 percent of group programs carpool using private passenger vehicles or Mass Audubon minivans. Approximately 50 percent of all participants who visit the Refuge as part of a Mass Audubon program travel on a school bus or other shared vehicle.

Several programs that take place on the Refuge include regular weekly bird watching programs on Wednesday morning (year-round), Wednesday evening, Saturday morning (seasonal), and Friday morning (May only). Almost all of these regular bird-watching programs, which do not require registration, bring visitors to the Refuge. The weekly programs have an average of 25 participants per session, although that average drops to approximately 18 participants during winter months and grows to as much as 45 participants during peak season. The participants are largely senior citizens with good mobility, although a few participants have limited mobility and are confined to their own vehicles. Often participants use their own vehicles, although Mass Audubon encourages carpooling and the use of seven-passenger Audubon vans.

Mass Audubon runs programs for school children and teachers throughout Essex County. Schools provide buses and also pay program fees to Mass Audubon, but Mass Audubon is limited in the number of groups that they can accommodate during the busy spring season. Mass Audubon brings educational programming to a local low-income assisted living center and to the Lowell Association for the Blind; the residents of the assisted living center and the Lowell Association do not have their own transportation. Mass Audubon charges reduced fees for these special-needs programs.[27]

Seasonality and Audubon Programs

The Joppa Flats Education Center runs educational programs year-round, with additional programs added during the peak birding season of late April through early June. A secondary peak occurs in September and October. Wednesday morning and Saturday morning birding programs run year-round, with peak attendance in the spring. Spring morning birding programs have up to 45 participants per session, compared to an average of 18 participants per session in the winter months. Additionally, Mass Audubon runs Friday morning birding sessions during the month of May only. Mass Audubon partners with Parker River NWR to run a bird banding station within Refuge boundaries where researchers gather data on species, age, sex, breeding characteristics, size, and weight. The station is open April, May, September, and October. School group visitation for field trips also peaks during these months as students participate in the bird banding program.

---

[27] Gette, Bill. 2011.

Special Events

Parker River NWR hosts several annual special events, which attract a total of about 3,500 visitors to the Refuge.[28] The Refuge hosts a few large events in conjunction with partners, and it hosts many smaller events using only Refuge staff and resources. Additionally, the Refuge could potentially participate in a number of local annual events and festivals that attract thousands of visitors to the northeastern Massachusetts area.

For larger events, the Refuge rents vehicles from Salter Transportation Inc. in Newbury. The cost of a school bus or a 24-passenger van rental is $565 per day, which includes a driver, fuel, and insurance. For some special events, such as the Eagle Festival, the Refuge provides funding to Mass Audubon as an event partner. Mass Audubon then uses these funds to rent buses, which is the single greatest expense for the festival. Special event vans and shuttles often run in loops to transport event participants to multiple sites associated with the event. For example, a shuttle may run a loop between the Refuge headquarters, Joppa Flats Education Center, Refuge boardwalks and trails, and downtown Newburyport.

Refuge staff noted several benefits in using large vehicles for special events or group tours. The vehicle allows for an interpretive guide to engage visitors throughout the tour and target sights during travel time. Opportunities for the Refuge staff to interact in person with visitors allow them to best educate the public on the unique wildlife and habitat within the Refuge. Refuge staff said that the use of a larger transit vehicle would also relieve traffic congestion that often accompanies programs and special events.[29]

The largest events are the Eagle Festival and the National Wildlife Refuge Week events. The Refuge currently leases transit vehicles for these events.

- The Merrimack River Eagle Festival takes place during one Saturday in mid-February each year, coinciding with the winter migration of bald eagles to the Merrimack River. Mass Audubon's Joppa Flats Education Center and the Refuge co-sponsor the event. The Festival includes guided eagle tours, led by volunteer naturalists; self-guided eagle viewing with interpretation by Audubon naturalists; live bird viewings; and children's activities. Festival events are located at locations in downtown Newburyport, the Joppa Flats Education Center, the Refuge Headquarters, and sites along the Merrimack River in Newburyport, Amesbury, and Newbury. Approximately 2,000 visitors attend the Saturday events of the Eagle Festival, with an additional 1,500 visitors coming to the area during the same week.
- Parker River celebrates National Wildlife Refuge Week (NWRW) with a one-day event in October, featuring a variety of activities to connect 1,500 visitors to Refuge resources and wildlife education. These activities include bird and wildlife exhibitors, wildlife artisans, a touch tank, and Refuge tours. The tours feature access to areas of the Refuge that are generally closed to the public. All events occur on Refuge facilities (at the Headquarters and within the Refuge). The Refuge hires one 24-passenger van from Salter Transportation Inc. from 9 a.m. to 4 p.m. and runs two tours throughout the day. The approximate VMT associated with this event is 30 to 50.[30]

---

[28] FWS Refuge Annual Performance Plan. 2011.
[29] Parker River National Wildlife Refuge Staff. 2011.
[30] Ibid.

Figure 16 – Use of Transit Vehicles at the Eagle Festival

Source: Volpe Center

The Refuge also hosts a number of smaller events throughout the year, as detailed in Table 9. Except where noted, Parker River NWR hosts all events listed on the top half of Table 9. Partner organizations host events on the bottom part of the table. The Refuge currently participates in many of the events hosted by partners, and Refuge staff recognize opportunities for future participation in the other events.

Table 9: Festivals and Special Events

Name of Event	Dates	Attendance	Vehicle Rental	Types of Programs	Location of Activities
Eagle Festival (co-hosted by Mass Audubon)	Mid-February (one day)	2,000 (one-day) 1,500 additional over the week of the festival	4 24-passenger vans 9 a m. – 4 p.m.	Naturalist tours, wildlife observation, educational programs, live demonstrations	Refuge headquarters, Joppa Flats Education Center, Newburyport City Hall, viewing sites along the Merrimack River
National Wildlife Refuge Week	October (one day)	1,500	1 24-passenger van 9 a m. – 4 p.m.	Refuge tours, exhibitors, carvers, touch tanks	Refuge headquarters, Refuge roads and trails (all on Refuge facilities); 2 tours daily
Go Fish	June (one day)	300 (approximate)	1 24-passenger van Noon – 6 p m	Fishing, children's programs	Refuge headquarters, Refuge beaches
Snowy Owl Program	February	Hundreds	Yes?	Refuge tours, naturalist interpretation	Refuge facilities
Open House at Great Bay NWR	June and September (one day each)		1 24-passenger van 9 a m. – 5 p.m.		Great Bay NWR
Biodiversity Day	June (one day)		None	Refuge and kayak tours; co-sponsored by the State of Massachusetts	Group tours on the Refuge
Beach Clean-Up Days	May and September (one day each)		None	Volunteer-based beach clean-up	Plum Island, Refuge beaches
Nature Photography Workshop	February (one day)		1 55-passenger school bus 7:30 a m. – 4 p m.	Co-sponsored by Essex National Heritage Area	
Gulf of Maine Institute Annual Conference	July (five days)		2-3 24-passenger vans 8 a m. – 5 p.m.	Formal Refuge partner organization	
Digital Nature Photography Day Camp	July (five days)		1 24-passenger van 7:30 a m.-5 p.m.		
Events Hosted by Partners					
Yankee Homecoming	Late July/ early August (10 days)	3,000 per day		Vendors, open stores, food Potential for Refuge tours from Newburyport	Downtown Newburyport
Trails & Sails	Mid-September (2 weekends)			Organized activities at natural and cultural areas throughout Essex Natural Heritage Area Refuge hosts kayak tour and guided hike Potential for Refuge tours from Newburyport	Essex Natural Heritage Area, downtown Newburyport, Refuge facilities
Riverfront Music Festival	July (2 days)		No	Music festival at Waterfront Park Potential for Refuge tours from Newburyport	Downtown Newburyport
Newburyport Buskers Festival	Labor Day Weekend (2 days)			Outdoor performance (musicians, jugglers) Potential for Refuge tours from Newburyport	Downtown Newburyport

Partners

Parker River NWR has a number of agencies and organizations that support the Refuge's management activities and that attract visitors to the Refuge. Parker River NWR employs a year-round staff of 11 and approximately 19 seasonal employees. The Refuge expands its capacity through partnering with other local, regional, and state organizations. Partners help to support environmental education and interpretive programs and special events, which tend to coincide with the highest periods of Refuge visitation and the greatest need for a transit vehicle. Partners are also important to draw additional funding and staff capacity for Refuge events, programs, and management activities. This section outlines the key actors and their capacity for assisting in the management and operations of a transit vehicle.

- **Mass Audubon:** Mass Audubon has a long history of conserving birds and habitat in Massachusetts. Joppa Flats was established in 1996, with the Education Center constructed in 2003 (in coordination with the construction of the Parker River Visitor Center in 2002). Mass Audubon and Parker River have shared a close relationship since Joppa Flats was established in 1996. The Refuge shares space and provides some funding to Mass Audubon for their bird banding efforts on the Refuge.

  Mass Audubon strongly supports the purchase of a transit vehicle, with the understanding that they would make use of the vehicle on a regular basis to bring educational program participants to the Refuge. Bill Gette, Director of Joppa Flats, noted that Mass Audubon could support a transit vehicle by participating or supporting funding applications, training staff to get commercial drivers' licenses to drive vehicles during programs and special events, and providing some assistance with cleaning and small-scale annual maintenance.

- **Massachusetts DCR:** DCR owns and manages Sandy Point Reservation at the southern end of the Refuge. DCR supports Refuge staff in closing access to the Refuge road (and consequently to Sandy Point) when the parking lots are full. DCR staff also recognizes the issues with congestion and parking within the Refuge and supports the use of a transit vehicle to enhance access for environmental education and interpretive programs during times of high use. DCR runs some interpretive programs at Sandy Point, including field trips, which could benefit from the use of a transit vehicle to minimize the number of cars associated with these programs.

- **Cities of Newburyport, Newbury, Rowley, Ipswich, and Salisbury:** Parker River NWR is located within four municipalities: Newbury, Newburyport, Rowley, and Ipswich. Visitors who use land-based travel modes to access the Refuge must pass through Newbury, Newburyport, or Rowley. In addition to maintaining infrastructure for access to the Refuge, municipalities can partner with the Refuge to attract new visitors to Refuge interpretive and environmental education programs. Municipalities can also benefit from increased patronage of their businesses from Refuge visitors.

  The City of Newburyport has been a close partner to the Refuge, in part because of the close proximity of the commercial activity center in downtown Newburyport. The Refuge partners with Newburyport for several special events and programs, such as working with students from Newburyport High School on an invasive species control program. Newburyport has a strong interest in reducing its greenhouse gas emissions and relieving parking congestion, which may align with Refuge goals for a transit vehicle. The City also has a new grant writer, in part to support new "green" initiatives. Newburyport's capacity for partnership also includes its Department of Public Services, which performs basic maintenance on a fleet of city-owned vehicles and has a trained mechanic on staff.

- **Merrimack Valley Regional Transit Authority:** The Merrimack Valley Regional Transit Authority (MVRTA) offers regional, fixed-route bus service to the municipalities of Andover, Amesbury, Haverhill, Lawrence, Merrimac, Methuen, Newburyport and North Andover. MVRTA also offers connections to the Lowell Transit Center and to downtown Boston. Route 51 offers service to the Newburyport commuter rail station, downtown Newburyport, and the Newburyport Park and Ride lot, with connections to Haverhill. Route 51 formerly included stops on Plum Island, but MVRTA eliminated the stops in 2007 due to low ridership and high costs. A seasonal bus route connecting Plum Island with the Newburyport Commuter Rail station and downtown was similarly eliminated. A "Ring and Ride" program currently offers on-demand van transit to Plum Island.

Existing Conditions Summary

Parker River NWR's visitation patterns and transportation needs fluctuate based on seasonal demands and constraints. The built environment accommodates seasonal variations in visitation, resource management, and species presence. Refuge management has established an inventory of vehicles, roads, parking lots, and buildings, as well as operational patterns, to accommodate current needs and conditions. The Refuge also works closely with its partners to manage Refuge visitation and enhance the Refuge staff's capacity.

Among the many characteristics of infrastructure, programs, operations, and management on the Refuge, several conditions most strongly support the need for a transit vehicle:

- High visitation in summer months and related Refuge closures preclude many visitors from enjoying wildlife-related recreational activities.
- Refuge roads and parking facilities are congested and may temporarily close during peak visitation periods. RAPP data shows an increase in Auto Tour visits, signaling a growing need to better manage traffic volume and patterns on Refuge roads.
- The Refuge has sufficient technical capacity to store, fuel, and maintain a transit vehicle.
- RAPP data shows strong and growing interest in interpretive and environmental education programs and special events.
- The Refuge's current passenger vehicles (a seven- and ten-passenger van) are often unavailable for interpretive and environmental education programs, especially during peak visitation season, and cannot accommodate larger group tours.
- The use of multiple, carpooling vehicles during environmental education and interpretive programs limits communication between participants and program guides.
- The Refuge works with several community partners to provide high quality programming and events throughout the year.

Given the infrastructure and programmatic conditions at Parker River NWR, a transit vehicle could help to enhance environmental education and interpretive programs on the Refuge while minimizing impacts to natural resources. The Refuge and its partners host special events, programs, and field trips throughout the year, including winter months, creating demand for a transit vehicle through all four seasons. The physical situation of the Refuge and the capacities of the Refuge and its partners indicate initial feasibility for a transit vehicle. The next section will apply data and current conditions to determine the optimal type of vehicle and service for the Refuge.

SECTION 3: DEMAND ANALYSIS

The existing conditions at the Refuge present management and resource challenges, several of which point to the need for a transit vehicle and service. The seasonality of parking, facility closures, and visitation patterns creates congestion and potential resource impacts, with particular management challenges during peak visitation and nesting seasons. This section translates the existing conditions at the Refuge into the potential demand for a transit vehicle that the Refuge would acquire. The demand includes the number of visitors who would participate in activities that utilize the vehicle and the number of miles the vehicle would travel annually.

For the demand analysis, the project team considers the Refuge's priorities of using an acquired transit vehicle primarily for programs and special events, as stated in conversations with Refuge staff. The project team also considers that the Refuge plans to actively pursue growth in program offerings when estimating future participation levels. Refuge management expressed the desire to increase and expand the scope of the Refuge's offerings of educational and interpretive programs. The Refuge has several Visitor Services staff to develop new educational and interpretive programs, with specific goals to create new programs for older students and adults.

As a secondary use, a transit vehicle with sufficient passenger capacity (25 or more) could be used as a shuttle to alleviate parking and road congestion challenges. During periods of parking restrictions, visitors or participants in group tours could park at the Refuge headquarters and board the bus for an interpretive tour. The bus could stop in closed parking areas to let passengers observe wildlife from observation towers or points, under the supervision of Refuge staff to ensure that visitors do not access restricted habitat areas.

Refuge Transportation Infrastructure Challenges

Transportation and access issues to and within the Refuge present several management challenges, most of which are beyond the scope of this Planning Study and may be addressed in a future Refuge comprehensive transportation study. These include carrying capacity, off-site parking, and transportation safety.

Within the scope of this Planning Study, the three most significant challenges for the Refuge related to transportation infrastructure are congestion in Refuge parking lots, congestion on Refuge Road and Sunset Drive, and speeding on Refuge Road (see Figure 1). Of these, Refuge staff notes that parking congestion occurs more frequently than congestion or speeding on Refuge Road. For the protection of sensitive species, such as piping plovers, the Refuge closes several parking lots seasonally (see Table 1). Between April and July, all beach access lots are closed, with the exception of lot 1 and Sandy Point lots. The Refuge's parking capacity is greatly reduced, and during days with warm weather, the open lots reach capacity quickly.

When all parking lots reach capacity, the gatehouse staff closes the Refuge to all vehicles, usually for several hours. The Refuge regularly experiences multiple closure events daily during summer weekends. During closure events, Refuge staff must turn away both recreational visitors and visitors interested in wildlife observation. Refuge staff closes the Refuge based on beach-access lot capacity, even during times that lots accessing wildlife observation areas have additional capacity, because they have no way to direct visitors specifically to wildlife observation areas. Staff expressed a desire to serve visitors interested in wildlife observation, if there were a way to do so without threatening species or creating additional burden for staff.

The second infrastructure challenge occurs as the Refuge experiences road congestion during periods of high visitation. Refuge Road becomes congested with the increased number of vehicles viewing wildlife or searching for limited parking spots. Additionally, closure events cause traffic queues of dozens of vehicles on Sunset Drive leading to the gatehouse, which increases air pollution, creates mobility challenges for Plum Island residents and employees, and upsets visitors, according to Refuge staff. Refuge staff also notes that drivers who find the Sandy Point lots at capacity often drop off passengers at Sandy Point and then shuttle vehicles to other refuge lots. The shuttling between lots both artificially fills refuge lots for non-refuge visitors and increases traffic on Refuge Road.

The third infrastructure challenge involves speeding vehicles, creating unsafe conditions for visitors and wildlife. Many vehicles drive above the speed limit of 25 miles per hour on summer mornings to reach the southern refuge lots or the Sandy Point lots before they reach capacity. High-speed driving carries safety risks for other vehicles, bicyclists, and pedestrians. It also increases the incidence of animal-vehicle collisions.

Transit Vehicle Demand Estimation

The vehicle selection and service planning are contingent upon an assessment of visitor demand for transit. The demand analysis consists of estimates of the number and types of users of the transit vehicle and the types and frequency of uses of the vehicle. The Existing Conditions analysis presents baseline data and conditions from which to estimate future demand for a transit vehicle.

Programs and Special Events

The Refuge's first goal for the transit feasibility study is to expand visitor opportunities for interpretation and environmental education. Refuge staff sees the primary use of a transit vehicle for interpretation and environmental education programs and special events. This section outlines the demand estimation for a transit vehicle for programs and special events, both in the short and long term, on the basis of Refuge staff feedback, current use patterns, and historic growth trends.

Baseline (2010) Estimation: Programs and Special Events
Currently, programs on the Refuge that rely upon vehicular transportation follow routes that range from 12 to 16 miles. These programs start at the Refuge headquarters (or at the Joppa Flats Education Center) and stop at one or more sites within the Refuge boundaries before returning back to the starting point. In a typical year, the Refuge staff estimates that they run 67 environmental education and interpretive programs that would benefit from the use of a transit vehicle (these vehicles currently rely mainly on private vehicles to transport participants). Mass Audubon estimates that it led 190 public programs that took place on the Refuge in 2010.[31] Given these estimates, and assuming a range of 12 to 16 VMT per program, a transit vehicle would run 3,084 to 4,112 miles per year for programs alone.

---

[31] The number of public programs does not include group programs, such as field trips or senior programs. Mass Audubon staff said that group programs typically provide their own vehicles, such as school buses, and would not generally need the use of a transit vehicle. Furthermore, the average size of group programs is 41 people, which would exceed the capacity of a transit vehicle. Therefore the demand analysis does not consider these group programs.

Additionally, Table 10 shows ten days of special events that the Refuge sponsors for which transit vehicles are currently used or would be used, upon availability. The table includes events that the Refuge currently hosts or participates, as well as events in the City of Newburyport and the Essex Natural Heritage Area that may benefit from structured programs led by Refuge staff. The total potential mileage from special events each year, as delineated in Table 10, is 1,388.

Table 10: Mileage for Special Events

Name of Event	Dates	Number of Vehicles Rented currently	Estimated Number of Trips	Miles Per Trip	Total Miles for Program
Eagle Festival (co-hosted by Mass Audubon)	Mid-February (one day)	4 24-passenger vans	12	8-12	96-144
National Wildlife Refuge Week	October (one day)	1 24-passenger van	2	16	32
Go Fish	June (one day)	1 24-passenger van	2	16	32
Snowy Owl Program	February	None	2	16	32
Open House at Great Bay NWR	June and September (one day each)	1 24-passenger van	1	60	60
Biodiversity Day	June (one day)	None	1	16	16
Beach Clean-Up Days	May and September (one day each)	None	2 (per day)	16	64
Nature Photography Workshop	February (one day)	1 55-passenger school bus	2	16	32
Events Hosted by Partners					
Yankee Homecoming (Newburyport)	Late July/ early August (10 days)	None	4 trips per weekend day and 2 trips per weekday; 28 total	16	448
Trails & Sails (Essex National Heritage Area)	Mid-September (two weekends)	None	4 trips per day	16	256
Riverfront Music Festival (Newburyport)	July (two days)	None	4 trips per day	16	128
Newburyport Buskers Festival	Labor Day Weekend (two days)	None	4 trips per day	16	128
TOTAL					1,388

Given 2010 visitation levels, the Refuge and its partners estimate that they could utilize a transit vehicle for the environmental education and interpretive programs and special events detailed above. At these use levels, the total VMT for a transit vehicle would be 4,472 to 5,500 miles per year.

Projected (2015 and 2020) Estimation: Programs and Special Events
Recent trends in visitation and participation in programs and special events indicate that the demand for these programs and events, and the related demand for transit vehicles to serve the events, is rising each year. The RAPP estimates of special event and program participants from 2006 through 2010 show a

general trend of increasing participation levels (see Table 7). While the number of special events remained consistent, the number of participants increased nearly threefold in four years, to 3,500 in 2010. Due to the increasing popularity of special events, the Refuge is considering new opportunities to offer Refuge tours in conjunction with the special events of their partners. For example, several of the events held in downtown Newburyport attract tens of thousands of visitors. A small percentage of these may enjoy a guided Refuge tour as part of their event experience, and the Refuge could use a transit vehicle to offer several tours during the event. According to RAPP estimates, the average annual increase in special event participation is approximately 550. If these trends continue, the Refuge would host approximately 6,264 participants in 2015 and 9,028 participants in 2020. The growth trends would be further supported by partnering with Newburyport for special events. Table 11 shows estimates for growth in events, environmental education, and interpretation programs, on the basis of historic growth.

The number of environmental education and interpretation participants increased between 2008 and 2009, with participation remaining above historic levels in 2010. For environmental education participants, the average annual increase in program participants is 68 (including a significant decrease in visitation between 2006 and 2007; the average over 2007 through 2010 is 460 participants per year). If the average annual increase in program participants from 2007 to 2010 continues at similar levels for the next ten years, the Refuge will have approximately 7,600 educational program participants in 2015 and 10,000 in 2020. As for interpretive programs, the average annual increase in participants has been 467, with an estimated 7,700 interpretive program participants in 2015 and nearly 10,000 in 2020. The Refuge has also expressed intentions of increasing its programmatic offerings, which would reinforce the participation increases.

Table 11: Estimated Growth in Program and Event Participation

Measure	Average # Change	2010	2015	2020
Number of participants in special events on site	550	3,500	6,300	9,000
Number of education participants involved in on- and off-site environmental education programs.	460	5,350	7,600	10,000
Number of interpretation participants in on- and off-site talks/programs	467	5,324	7,700	10,000

Source: RAPP data and Volpe Center estimates

If the increases in program and event participation continue at similar rates through 2020, as predicted by visitation patterns since 2006, the Refuge may see demand for programs double and demand for special events nearly triple.[32] The VMT for a transit vehicle may range from 6,300 to 7,900 miles per year by 2020.

---

[32] For the purposes of estimating demand, this analysis assumes that the Refuge may increase its program offerings by 50 percent by 2020. In that case, the VMT for a transit vehicle would be 4,626 to 6,168 for interpretation and environmental education programs. This estimate is based on the current VMT estimate for these programs of 3,084 to 4,112 miles per year multiplied by 150 percent. This analysis assumes a more modest increase in special event attendance, given that the current estimate of 1,388 miles already includes several new events from the City of Newburyport. The assumed increase in VMT for special events is 25 percent (125 percent of 1,388 miles), for a total of 1,735 VMT. Therefore, by 2020 the Refuge could realistically expect a transit vehicle to cover 6,361 to 7,903 miles per year.

General Refuge Visitation: Baseline and Growth Projection

Refuge staff expects program and special event participation to be the most significant drivers of transit vehicle demand. However, the conditions presented through general visitation levels contribute to the need for a transit vehicle as well. Heavy use of the Refuge for beach recreation leads to congestion, parking constraints, pollution, resource impacts, and Refuge closures. While most of the impacts are related to recreational use, a transit vehicle could alleviate each of these impacts, to a small degree, by redirecting some visitor travel for wildlife observation and photography.

Overall visitation levels at the Refuge have fluctuated between 2008 and 2010, with an average of approximately 260,000 annual visitors over that time period. From 2005 to 2007, the availability of visitation data, which is calculated from vehicle entry through the gatehouse, was limited due to a malfunctioning traffic counter. The data does not indicate any strong trends to predict future visitation. However, continuous high visitation levels, especially during spring and summer months, indicates that the Refuge can reasonably expect to see visitation around the current levels in the near future. If visitation levels stay consistent, the Refuge will continue to experience frequent closures during peak visitation periods.

The Refuge has not formally measured its carrying capacity for visitation, which would include the capacity of both its built infrastructure (such as roads and buildings) and impacts to habitat areas. Instead, the Refuge uses parking capacity as a proxy measure for carrying capacity of the Refuge. Refuge staff acknowledge that this measure is imperfect, as some wildlife observation facilities could accommodate additional visitors during times that beach access parking lots are full. At current visitation levels, the Refuge exceeds its parking capacity on a regular basis due to beach recreation users. The Refuge closes its facilities several times a day during peak summer weekends, and some weekdays. If visitation levels remain consistent or rise in the future, the Refuge will continue to exceed its parking capacity frequently.

Refuge staff want to be cautious of attracting greater visitation, recognizing the potential natural resource impacts associated with heavy visitation. These impacts stem from the activities of visitors and from the impacts of their vehicles. Increased numbers of visitors increases human foot traffic on sensitive habitat areas, litter, and noise levels, among other impacts. Visitor vehicles increase air pollution, impact water and soils through stormwater runoff from roads, and raise noise levels. The current frequency of days in which visitation exceeds parking capacity signifies the frequency of potential threats to the Refuge's natural resources.

With consistent or growing visitation and limited parking capacity, the Refuge will need to pursue new ways to manage visitor use and natural resource protection. The use of a transit vehicle to displace personal vehicles could reduce the resource impacts resulting from visitor-owned vehicles. A 28-passenger transit van could replace up to 11 private vehicles (based on an average occupancy of 2.4 people per vehicle) per program or event, thereby helping the Refuge stay within its carrying capacity. Refuge staff or volunteers (or staff from partner agencies) would always accompany transit vehicle passengers as program leaders or tour guides. The participation of staff and volunteers would result in a greater likelihood that these visitors would refrain from activities that negatively impact natural resources.

Transit Vehicle Demand: Impacts and Benefits

As described in previous sections, a transit vehicle can assist the Refuge in expanding visitor program opportunities, reducing congestion, and protecting natural resources. The magnitude of these benefits would depend, on large part, on the demand for and the use of the transit vehicle. The project team estimates that a transit vehicle would have an annual VMT of approximately 4,500 to 5,500, using 2010 visitation levels. The VMT could grow to 6,300 to 7,900 by 2020.

The estimates of transit vehicle use are contingent upon several factors, including the following:

- Consistency in growth of program and special event participation;
- New program offerings from the Refuge and its partners;
- Refuge participation in special events; and
- Visitor participation rates in programs that use a transit vehicle.

The quantifiable benefits to the Refuge would include growth in program participation, cars removed from Refuge roads and parking lots, and VMT reduction.[33] The most significant variables in determining the impact of a transit vehicle would be the percentage of programs that utilized the vehicle and the accuracy of growth estimates in program and special event participation.

Tables 12, 13, and 14 outline the potential reductions in vehicles on the Refuge and in VMT associated with the use of a transit vehicle. The tables consider estimated growth from 2010 to 2020 and the percentage of total Refuge programs that would utilize a transit vehicle.

The Tables demonstrate a significant range in impact based on program and special event participation levels and the percentage of programs that use the transit vehicle. The Refuge can exercise direct control over the percentage of programs that use the transit vehicle by requiring program participants to use the transit vehicle instead of their personal automobiles. They can also require partner agencies to do the same for their programs. Not all of the Refuge's programs or special event offerings are compatible with transit vehicle use, depending on the size of the program or event and the amount of travel involved. At the low end of the spectrum, with only 25 percent of programs and events utilizing the vehicle, the Refuge would still reduce VMT by over 20,000 miles annually based on current visitation levels. The Refuge could potentially reduce VMT by as much as 62,000 miles per year, based on current visitation levels and 75 percent utilization rates.

Refuge staff can also encourage participation in Refuge programs by expanding the number and types of program and special event offerings, which would help ensure that average annual increase in program participants remain steady through the next decade. Assuming growth rates follow existing trends, the VMT reductions would range from 42,000 to 127,000 by 2020.

The estimated quantifiable benefits to the Refuge can also serve as indicators for other benefits, such as reduced fuel use and air pollution, reduced impacts on sensitive habitat areas, and enhanced visitor education and experience. The Refuge would have to take an active management role to realize these benefits. To achieve maximum results from a vehicle purchase, Refuge staff should expand program offerings, promote the use of the transit vehicle for all feasible programs and special events, and work closely with partners to maximize the use of the vehicle for partner-led programs and events.

---

[33] Estimates of cars removed from roads and parking lots is based on the number of participants divided by the Refuge's average vehicle occupancy rate of 2.4 persons per vehicle. VMT reduction estimates are based on the number of vehicles removed multiplied by an average trip length for programs of 14 miles (accounting for the VMT of the transit vehicle).

Table 12: Impacts of the Use of a Transit Vehicle for 25 Percent of Refuge Programs

Measure	2010				2015				2020			
	Participants	Participants in Transit Vehicles	Cars Removed	VMT Reduced	Participants	Participants in Transit Vehicles	Cars Removed	VMT Reduced	Participants	Participants in Transit Vehicles	Cars Removed	VMT Reduced
Special event participants	3,500	875	365	5,090	6,264	1,566	653	9,121	9,028	2,257	940	13,152
Environmental education program participants	5,350	1,338	557	7,788	7,648	1,912	797	11,139	9,947	2,487	1,036	14,492
Interpretive program participants	5,324	1,331	555	7,750	7,660	1,915	798	11,157	9,997	2,499	1,041	14,565

Table 13: Impacts of the Use of a Transit Vehicle for 50 Percent of Refuge Programs

Measure	2010				2015				2020			
	Participants	Participants in Transit Vehicles	Cars Removed	VMT Reduced	Participants	Participants in Transit Vehicles	Cars Removed	VMT Reduced	Participants	Participants in Transit Vehicles	Cars Removed	VMT Reduced
Special event participants	3,500	1,750	729	10,194	6,264	3,132	1,305	18,256	9,028	4,514	1,881	26,318
Environmental education program participants	5,350	2,675	1,115	15,590	7,648	3,824	1,593	22,293	9,947	4,974	2,072	28,998
Interpretive program participants	5,324	2,662	1,109	15,514	7,660	3,830	1,596	22,328	9,997	4,999	2,083	29,144

Table 14: Impacts of the Use of a Transit Vehicle for 75 Percent of Refuge Programs

Measure	2010				2015				2020			
	Participants	Participants in Transit Vehicles	Cars Removed	VMT Reduced	Participants	Participants in Transit Vehicles	Cars Removed	VMT Reduced	Participants	Participants in Transit Vehicles	Cars Removed	VMT Reduced
Special event participants	3,500	2,625	1,094	15,299	6,264	4,698	1,958	27,391	9,028	6,771	2,821	39,484
Environmental education program participants	5,350	4,013	1,672	23,392	7,648	5,736	2,390	33,446	9,947	7,460	3,108	43,504
Interpretive program participants	5,324	3,993	1,664	23,279	7,660	5,745	2,394	33,499	9,997	7,498	3,124	43,723

Source: RAPP 2010 and Volpe Center estimates

Conclusions

The current growth in participation for Refuge programs and special events, combined with the existing infrastructure and congestion challenges that the Refuge faces, indicate a strong demand for a transit vehicle. A vehicle used primarily for programs and special events would have relatively low levels of use in terms of mileage but could have a positive impact in terms of overall VMT in the Refuge and visitor experience. Refuge staff can directly and indirectly manage several variables that could improve the benefits associated with a transit vehicle, such as actively enhancing and promoting program and special event offerings and requiring future programs and events to use the vehicle, where possible.

SECTION 4: VEHICLE ANALYSIS

The project team explored acquisition of a transit vehicle that would meet the Refuge's needs, as defined through the existing conditions and demand analysis. The vehicle analysis includes acquisition mechanisms, types of vehicles and options, vehicle costs, fuel options, and maintenance considerations. The vehicle analysis focuses on the purchase of a new vehicle from the General Services Administration (GSA), but the analysis also includes considerations for leasing and used vehicle purchase.

Vehicle Capacity

The existing conditions and demand analysis sections of this report and interviews with Refuge staff indicated that the Refuge should consider several key factors in selecting an appropriate vehicle to best suit the Refuge's needs.

The first consideration factor is vehicle passenger capacity, which is based on the anticipated primary use of the vehicle for programs and special events. Table 10 identifies vehicle needs to accommodate visitation to the Refuge for current and future special events. With two exceptions (the Eagle Festival and the Nature Photography Workshop), a single, 24-passenger van rental can meet visitation needs for these events. For events and programs hosted by partners, the Refuge and partner organization staff use existing vehicles (Mass Audubon's three seven-passenger vans and the Refuge's seven and ten-passenger van) or personal vehicles. Mass Audubon reports that the average size of its regular group birding programs (such as Wednesday morning birding) ranges from 18 to 25 participants, depending on the season.[34] Therefore, the Refuge could accommodate these events and programs with a 28-passenger van.

In the medium-duty shuttle bus category, GSA restricts passenger capacities to three sizes: 28-, 32- and 36-passenger. In the light-duty shuttle bus category, GSA has a low-floor and high-floor option with a 28-passenger capacity.[35] (The evaluation considered and eliminated the light-duty, low-floor option, as the cost significantly exceeded the cost of a medium-duty vehicle.) The remaining analysis and vehicle selection process will focus exclusively on the light-duty high-floor and medium-duty options available in the 28-passenger range.

Vehicle Options

The Federal Acquisition Regulation (FAR) requires FWS to purchase vehicles through the GSA. The GSA's Schedules Program serves as the basis for federal agencies to quickly and efficiently award purchase contracts to vendors who provide "fair and reasonable" pricing, and also ensure that purchases are Buy America compliant (required by CFR Title 49, Chapter VI - Part 661). The GSA released their 2011 Vehicle Schedule in March of 2011; vehicles, options, pricing and availability are valid through March of 2012. A GSA representative indicated that the current schedule is a multi-year contract and

---

[34] The programs occasionally attract up to 45 participants, but the project team would not recommend the purchase of a vehicle to accommodate these infrequent programs. Instead, the Refuge should consider and accommodate average group sizes, accompanied by Refuge or Mass Audubon passenger vans during programs with anticipated high attendance.

[35] Low-floor option vehicles allow for easier access for wheelchairs and mobility-impaired passengers, without the use of a wheelchair lift. Due to the high cost of these vehicles and the lack of curbed infrastructure within the Refuge, they would not be a logical choice for the Refuge.

pricing is unlikely to increase for the subsequent year. However, manufacturers may eliminate or update available models and options, which would impact pricing and availability.

GSA offers 28-passenger shuttle buses in both the light-duty and medium-duty categories. The light-duty shuttle buses have V8 diesel engines with chassis and drivetrain combinations that are designed for low-mileage daily use of passenger transport. These vehicles also have capacity for occasional heavy-duty tasks, such as hauling materials. The medium-duty shuttle buses are equipped with V6 diesel engines; these vehicles are designed to operate more demanding transit schedules with greater daily mileage, significant grades, and/or high-traffic urban routes.[36] Both vehicles can meet the Refuges' needs for transit, based on the anticipated low mileage and flat grades of the anticipated vehicle routes. The medium-duty vehicle may offer benefits in terms of long-term service reliability and capacity to handle greater mileage and loads without maintenance, but the vehicles are more expensive than light-duty vehicles. The light-duty vehicles can meet the Refuge's basic needs while saving money on purchase costs.

Light-Duty Vehicles

The GSA Schedule includes three options in the light-duty shuttle bus range: the Glaval Entourage F550, the Startrans Senator HD, and the Champbus Challenger F550. All options are equipped with V8 diesel engines rated at a minimum of 300 horsepower (HP) and 600 pounds-feet (lb. ft) of torque. The GSA does not provide fuel economy specifications for any of the available options. Figures 17, 18, and 19 show photographs of each light-duty vehicle.

The light-duty options are equipped with V8 diesel engines paired with OEM transmissions. Each of the three light-duty options carries a good reliability reputation. The engine and transmission combination is not designed to be as robust or perform under the same operating conditions as the medium-duty vehicle, but the light-duty options would still feasibly meet the Refuge's long-term needs.

Figure 17 - Glaval Entourage F550

---

[36] Although the light-duty vehicles have more cylinders in their engines than the medium-duty vehicles, the engine displacement remains the same at 6.7 liters. The medium-duty vehicle has both an engine and a chassis that are designed to provide more robust and heavy-duty service. Fewer cylinders (of greater displacement per cylinder) results in greater low-end torque, allowing the engine to reach maximum power at lower engine speeds (RPMs). Conversely, the light-duty engine and chassis combination are designed for use in large trucks, rather than for high-mileage transit uses and the V8-equipped light-duty engine will reach its maximum power and torque at higher RPMs. The V6 engine will therefore move an equivalent load at lower RPMs, effectively lessening the load on the engine and associated components. Both engines would be appropriate for the anticipated use levels on the Refuge.

Figure 18 – Startrans Senator HD

Figure 19 - ChampBus Challenger F550

Source: GSA

The GSA does not offer fuel economy ratings for the light-duty vehicles. However, a similar model to one of the buses (the Glaval Entourage) has been through FTA's Altoona Bus Testing program, which includes the provision of fuel economy measurements.[37] The Altoona program is a testing program that all vehicles must pass to be eligible for purchase by transit agencies that use matching funds from the FTA for fleet vehicle purchases. The FTA report states that the average idle consumption of 0.38 gallons per hour, average business district consumption of 6.58 mpg and an average arterial consumption of 6.69.[38] The bus that was tested featured the engine noted above in a conventional (non-hybrid) drivetrain and fueled by ultra-low sulfur diesel (ULSD) fuel. Hybrid data is not available for any light-duty vehicle at the time of publication (more description about fuel economy and drivetrain options appear later in this section). Depending on the amount of idling during use at the Refuge, a light-duty vehicle equipped with the standard diesel option should have an average fuel economy of approximately 6.6 miles per gallon.

The GSA offers two levels of equipment options in the light-duty category, "Basic" and "Standard." Features included in the standard option include:

---

[37] The tested bus is the 33 foot model, the largest in the Glaval Entourage line.
[38] The Thomas D. Larson Penn State Transportation Research Institute. 2010. Partial STURAA (The Surface Transportation and Uniform Relocation Assistance Act of 1987) Test, 7 Year 200,000 Mile Bus from Glaval Bus Model 33' Entourage. PTI-BT-R1012-P.

- Public address system integrated with the radio
- Bright white exterior paint
- Remote controlled and heated exterior mirrors
- Interior walls and ceiling padded with grey cloth or carpet surface to aid in noise reduction
- Fluorescent overhead interior lighting
- Light-emitting diode (LED) exterior lighting
- Daytime running lights
- Individual mid-high seats with grey cloth upholstery
- Medium grey color 2.2 millimeter thick Altro transit flooring (durable flooring)
- Transit style tinted passenger windows
- Coolant system equipped with constant tension hose clamps and extended life coolant
- Engine block heater
- Heated rearview mirrors
- Tilt steering wheel
- Improved ride quality (suspension)

The standard option comes with several included features that are not included with the basic option. Several of these features are important to achieve the Refuge's goals for transit vehicle use and the "standard" option provides value for these options. Based on anticipated program use and operating conditions, the Refuge would need a vehicle that includes a public-address system, durable flooring (for ease of cleaning) and fabric wall lining and seating options (fabric interior covering helps to reduce vehicle noise). The Refuge should select the "standard" option for purchase.

Available options for the standard option light-duty bus, which are not included in the basic option, include:

- Coolant heater – fuel fired
- Limited slip differential
- Automatic traction assist
- On board battery charger
- Master disconnect battery switch
- **Custom color paint**
- Heated entry step
- Rear loading door
- Bottom vent transit slider
- Passenger door – sedan type
- Passenger fixed touring windows
- Destination sign (roller, front)
- Destination sign (roller, side)
- Destination sign (electric, front)
- Destination sign (electric, side)
- Individually controlled reading lights
- Backup video camera (dash mounted)
- Security video camera package

- Video viewing and DVD packages
- Standee grab rails
- **Interior overhead parcel racks**
- Rack luggage options
- Interior baggage compartments
- Movable storage walls
- Flat flooring w/o wheel intrusion
- Carpeted floor covering
- Various seat configurations and fabric options
- **Wheelchair lift packages and restraint systems**
- Fire suppression systems and warning lights
- Air suspension
- Tire pressure monitoring systems
- Various spare tire assemblies
- Surround passenger seating

While many of the equipment options may offer some benefit to the Refuge, there are a few options that would be of greatest need for the Refuge, on the basis of its physical environment and operational needs. These options are highlighted in bold above, explained in more detail below, and summarized in Table 15.

- Overhead parcel racks, a wheelchair lift and wheelchair restraint can accommodate visitors of all mobility levels and will meet requirements of the Americans with Disabilities Act (ADA)[39].
- Custom color paint would help to ensure that visitors and the public recognize the Refuge's logo and color scheme in association with the vehicle.

Other options such as traction assist and limited-slip differentials would not be useful in the Refuge's operating environment, which is essentially a flat road with paved and gravel sections. Manufacturer's standard equipment is anticipated to meet the needs of the Refuge both within their boundaries and on surrounding highways (including for travel to other regional refuges), as all standard equipment is highway compliant.

Medium-Duty Vehicles

The GSA Schedule includes four models in the medium-duty shuttle bus range: the Glaval Concord II (F650), Startrans Tourliner Freightliner, the IC Bus HC, and the Turtle Top Odyssey XL (see Figures 20 to 23 for photographs of each vehicle). All options are equipped with a conventional diesel power plant, with each utilizing a diesel engine in an inline, six-cylinder layout rated at 240 horsepower (HP) and 560

---

[39] ADA compliant wheelchair lifts require appropriate clear space (30 inches by 48 inches) for deployment of the lift at passenger pick up and drop off areas. The Refuge may wish to consider construction of a wayside platform to allow for clear space and level loading at the Refuge headquarters.

pounds-feet (lb. ft) of torque. The GSA does not provide fuel economy specifications for any vehicle except for the IC Bus (rated at six to eight miles per gallon).[40] The Glaval Concorde II has been through the FTA Altoona Bus Testing program, and the FTA report recorded an average idle consumption of 0.55 gallons per hour, average business district consumption of 5.42 mpg and an average arterial consumption of 6.24.[41] The bus that was tested featured the engine noted above in a conventional (non-hybrid) drivetrain and fueled by conventional ULSD fuel. To date, no hybrid has been through Altoona bus testing and fuel economy data is not available. Depending on the amount of idling during use at the Refuge, a medium-duty vehicle equipped with the standard diesel option should have an average fuel economy of approximately 5.8 miles per gallon.

Figure 20 - Startrans Tourliner

Figure 21 - Turtle Top Odyssey XL

[40] U.S. General Services Administration. 2011. GSA Autochoice. Accessed 9 May 2011: http://www.gsa.gov/portal/content/100012.
[41] The Thomas D. Larson Penn State Transportation Research Institute. 2007. STURAA Test, 10 Year 350,000 Mile Bus from Glaval Bus Model 40' Concorde II. PTI-BT-R0703.

Figure 22 – IC Bus HC

Figure 23 - Glaval Concord II

Source: GSA

The diesel engine and transmission combination equipped as standard in all the vehicle options (excluding the hybrid option) are heavy-duty diesels paired with heavy-duty transmissions and carry an excellent reliability reputation.[42] Any of these vehicles could feasibly meet the Refuge's long-term needs.

The GSA Schedule offers two options for each medium-duty bus: "basic" and "standard." The "standard" option ranges from $10,000 to $14,000 above the price of the "basic" option and includes the following features:

- Engine block heater
- Heated fuel-water separator

---

[42] The medium-duty vehicles will have greater overall reliability over the life of the vehicle, as compared with the light-duty vehicles. However, the light-duty vehicles will be sufficiently reliable to meet the Refuge's needs.

- Tinted and tempered passenger windows
- Light-emitting diode (LED) exterior lighting
- Daytime running lights
- Public address system
- Energy saving interior lighting
- Tilt steering wheel
- One piece vinyl transit grade flooring (medium gray)
- Padded woven fabric surface walls (medium gray)
- Padded woven fabric surface ceiling (medium gray)
- Track-mounted seating
- Fabric woven grey cloth seat covering (vinyl on basic)
- Air + Spring Suspension (air adjustable suspension)[43]

Several features included in the "standard" vehicle would be important to achieve the Refuge's goals for transit vehicle use. Based on anticipated program use and operating conditions, the Refuge would need a vehicle that includes a public-address system, an engine block heater, a heated fuel-water separator, and fabric wall lining and seating options (fabric interior covering helps to reduce vehicle noise). Specifically, the engine block heater and the fuel-water separator would increase fuel economy and operational efficiency during cold weather months. Given the need for these features, the Refuge should select the "standard" option for vehicle purchase.

Available optional equipment for the standard option bus, which are not included in the basic option, includes:
- **Two-stage air cleaner**
- Fuel-fired coolant heater
- Automated manual transmission
- Air brakes
- Air & disc brakes
- Automatic transmission integrated braking retarded
- Engine exhaust brake
- OEM all wheel drive
- Limited slip differential
- On-board battery charger
- Master switch – battery disconnect
- Under-floor storage compartments (minimum 20, and 40 cubic feet options)
- **Custom color paint**
- Heated door entry step
- Rear loading door
- Sedan-type passenger door
- Transit slider passenger window
- Destination signage
- Reading lights
- Back-up and security video camera systems
- Video monitors w/ DVD/VCR player
- Standee grab rails, **overhead parcel racks**, baggage compartment and storage walls
- Lavatory
- Flat floor w/o wheel-arch intrusions
- Carpeted floor

---

[43] GSA 2011.

- Roof mounted A/C condenser
- Mechanical or air driver & co-pilot seating suspensions
- Various seating and fabric options
- **Wheelchair lift packages & restraint systems**
- Energy absorbing bumpers
- Fire suppression system
- Tire pressure monitoring system (TPMS)
- Parts and Service manuals

While many of the equipment options may offer some benefit to the Refuge, there are a few options that would be of greatest need for the Refuge, on the basis of its physical environment and operational needs. These options are highlighted in bold above, explained in more detail below, and summarized in Table 16.

- Overhead parcel racks, a wheelchair lift and wheelchair restraint can accommodate visitors of all mobility levels and will meet requirements of the Americans with Disabilities Act (ADA).
- Custom color paint would help to ensure that visitors and the public recognize the Refuge's logo and color scheme in association with the vehicle.
- A two-stage air cleaner could remove air particulates such as sea salt or sand associated with the seaside operating environment. However, this option is not available from all manufacturers and will not be included in the build-options mentioned in the following section (to present a more accurate comparison).

Other options such as enhanced brakes, all-wheel drive, and limited-slip differentials would not be useful in the Refuge's operating environment, which is essentially a flat road with paved and gravel sections. Manufacturer standard equipment is anticipated to meet the needs of the Refuge both within their boundaries and on surrounding highways (including for travel to other regional refuges), as all standard equipment is highway compliant.

Vehicle Pricing

The manufacturer base price for all standard option vehicles, without optional equipment, is as follows:

Light Duty

- $81,422 – Glaval Entourage F550
- $83,235 – Startrans Senator HD
- $84,127 – ChampBus Challenger F550

Table 15: GSA Available Optional Equipment Cost Summary (Light Duty)

Option Description	Glaval	Startrans	ChampBus
Interior Overhead Parcel Racks (LRI)	$1,100	$825	$1,485
Paint Custom Color (PCC)	N/A	$2,310	$2,200
Maxon Wheelchair Lift Package (WCL1)	$4,822	$4,516	$4,715
Wheelchair Occupant Restraint (WORQ)	$395	$982	$1,220

Source: GSA Autochoice 2011

Medium Duty:

- $106,549.00 – Glaval Concord II
- $121,455.00 – Startrans Tourliner
- $125,597.00 – IC Bus HC
- $127,625.00 – Turtle Top Odyssey XL

Table 16: GSA Available Optional Equipment Cost Summary (Medium Duty)

Option Description	Glaval	Startrans	IC Bus HC	Turtle Top
Interior Overhead Parcel Racks (LRI)	$1,100	$853	$1,400	$1,570
Paint Custom Color (PCC)	$2,600	$2,530	$2,000	$5,035
Maxon Wheelchair Lift Package (WCL1)	$4,832	$4,692	$4,250	$5,033
Wheelchair Occupant Restraint (WORQ)	$395	$982	$100	$1,111
Diesel Engine (YD3A)	$0	$198	$223	$798

Source: GSA Autochoice 2011

Configured with the recommended options from Tables 15 and 16, the cost per vehicle amounts to:

Light Duty

- $88,623.89 – Glaval Entourage F550
- $92,799.42 – Startrans Senator HD
- $94,695.47 – ChampBus Challenger F550

Medium Duty

- $116,620.66 – Glaval Concord II
- $132,017.10 – Startrans Tourliner
- $134,905.70 – IC Bus HC
- $142,583.72 – Turtle Top Odyssey XL

Each of the above vehicles will meet the Refuge's basic needs and would be a viable option for purchase.[44] Federal regulations require federal agencies to purchase the least-expensive vehicle that can meet their needs, or to submit a waiver explaining the need for a higher-cost vehicle. Therefore, the Refuge would need to purchase the Glaval Entourage F550 for a light-duty option, the Glaval Concord II for the medium-duty option, or submit a waiver with justification for the purchase of a different vehicle.

Vehicle Fueling Options

The medium-duty options discussed in this report all pair a heavy-duty diesel engine with a reliable heavy-duty automatic transmission. In addition to this conventional drivetrain pairing, the Turtle Top, Startrans Tourliner, and IC Bus HC are offered with a hybrid-drive option. The addition of hybrid-drive adds $63,940, $68,486, and $80,644 to the sale price, respectively. Two of the light-duty options are also available with a hybrid-drive option. The Glaval Entourage and the Startrans Senator have a hybrid option for a cost of $38,756 and $48,997, respectively, in addition to their base prices. [45]

Given the anticipated VMT range of 4,472-7,900 miles per year (with the VMT increasing over time based on expanded program offerings, as discussed in the demand analysis section), a hybrid-drive option would not likely recoup the initial costs of a hybrid-drive system through fuel savings (fuel consumption combined with fuel cost). For example, a 50,000-mile expected ten-year life with a fuel efficiency of 6.0 miles per gallon would result in approximately 8,300 gallons of fuel consumed over ten years. If the hybridization of the drivetrain resulted in a 30 to 50 percent fuel economy gain,[46] the vehicle would have an average fuel efficiency of 7.8 to 9.0 miles per gallon average and consume 5,500 to 6,400 gallons of fuel over the same ten-year period. At an assumed average fuel cost of $4 per gallon, the increased fuel efficiency would result in less than $12,000 worth of fuel savings over the ten-year life. With major increases in the cost of fuel of up to $10 per gallon, the savings would reach as much as $30,000 but still not meet the incremental costs of a hybrid-drive system for a light-duty or a medium-duty vehicle.

Without dramatic increases in total VMT expectations, a financial-based argument fails to outweigh the increased cost associated with a hybrid option. The Refuge may still consider a hybrid option to address its goal of leadership in environmental stewardship. The hybrid option would moderately reduce greenhouse gas emissions and other pollutants and reduce vehicle noise within the Refuge due to the quieter noise levels of the hybrid vehicle. The total cost of a light-duty vehicle with a hybrid-drive option would be approximately $127,000 for the Glaval Entourage or $138,650 for the Startrans Senator; both would be in the same price range as the non-hybrid medium-duty vehicles.[47] The Refuge may decide to invest in the hybrid option to demonstrate environmental leadership and achieve some fuel savings.

The standard diesel engine option is compatible with a light biodiesel blend consisting of five percent biodiesel (B5). Additionally, the GSA notes that all medium-duty shuttle vehicles are compatible with a twenty percent (B20) blend. Both B5 and B20 blends have been shown to reduce emissions and aid in reliability. Agencies operating in similar climates will often utilize such a blend year-round; however, switching between biodiesel blends and ULSD can be made at any time and in any percentage blend both in-vehicle and in-tank (e.g.: B5 and ULSD can be utilized independently or blended together). The project team recommends the use of a B20 blend during warm-weather months and a B10 or B5 blend during cooler-weather months. Both blends have been found to increase the lubricity of the fuel, leading to lower wear-and-tear on mechanical items within the fuel system (fuel pumps, fuel lines, injectors, etc.).

As the Refuge considers the fuel type for a transit vehicle, it should use the options available through GSA, which will serve the Refuge's needs while allowing the potential to fuel with a light biodiesel blend. The vehicle would not require modification to run a light five-percent biodiesel blend, allowing the Refuge the ability to operate the vehicle with its existing fueling infrastructure, and to either expand its fueling capabilities with an additional fuel tank or switch its entire diesel fleet to biodiesel blends at a

---

[45] GSA 2011.

[46] There is limited data availability on the GSA vehicles for hybrid-drive option fuel economy. One source for the IC Bus HC noted that their hybrid bus had a fuel efficiency improvement of 32 percent over the conventional bus. Another research study from the National Renewable Energy Laboratory found up to 45 percent improvements in fuel efficiency in hybrid buses over conventional buses.
ICBus. 2011. HC Series Hybrid Overview. Accessed 1 June 2011:
http://www.icbus.com/ICBus/Buses/Commercial/Overview/Commercial+HC+Hybrid/.
Green Car Congress. 2006. "NYC Hybrid Buses Improve Fuel Economy 45% Over Diesel, 100% Over CNG." Accessed 1 June 2011:
http://www.greencarcongress.com/2006/02/nyc_hybrid_buse.html

[47] The GSA only prices hybrid-drive options for the basic option light-duty vehicles. The project team recommends the purchase of standard option vehicles, which include wheelchair lifts and custom paint. However, if the Refuge chooses to purchase a hybrid-drive light-duty vehicle, staff could add the recommended options onto the basic hybrid vehicle, which may slightly increase the total price of the vehicle.

later time.[48] Finally, the project team recommends that the Refuge consider the relative priority of its environmental leadership goals to determine if the purchase of a hybrid vehicle can be justified, given the anticipated, limited annual VMT for the vehicle.

Vehicle Maintenance Considerations

The Refuge has capabilities to carry out some of the scheduled and preventative maintenance (PM) and facilitate major repairs on a new shuttle vehicle. Most major servicing will be performed by nearby service centers. Authorized service centers will also be able to perform manufacturer recalls and warranty repair; however warranty terms will vary by manufacturer and may permit vehicle service from local service providers.

The Refuge should consider its own existing capabilities and resources in planning for the maintenance needs of a new vehicle. Given the nature of the Refuge's road (less than seven miles long with little change in elevation) and anticipated routes (generally 15 miles round trip), the physical demand and wear and tear on the vehicle will be relatively minimal. An annual or six-month service incorporating scheduled service items, PM items, and an annual inspection should meet the requirements for a new vehicle operating within the anticipated duty cycles at the Refuge. Based on existing regulations, the vehicle may require inspection for specific safety items more frequently than general servicing and PM intervals. Some safety items may require 90-day inspection intervals.[49] The Refuge should have sufficient technical resources to accommodate required periodic inspections on-site (Section VI contains information on maintenance costs).

Manufacturer recommended service schedules, industry standard PM procedures, and applicable federal safety regulations should serve as a baseline for establishing a vehicle specific service schedule. The service schedules provided by the manufacturer will include vehicle specific maintenance items and will include the recommended maintenance intervals for the diesel engines as optioned in the vehicles noted in this report. Engine-specific service intervals are measured in hours. Table 17 lists a sample maintenance schedule for a Cummins HD diesel engine, similar to those found in the listed vehicle options.[50] While the Cummins 6.7L engine more closely resembles those of the medium-duty vehicles, the service intervals should be approximately similar for light-duty vehicles, given the anticipated level of use. Due to the anticipated total hours of vehicle use, the 500 hour service interval would need to be performed once or twice per year. If the vehicle were to be utilized for longer-duration programs and or idle frequently, it may require more frequent servicing. In either event, Refuge staff should record hours of vehicle operation for maintenance planning.

---

[48] The Refuge could also use up to a B20 blend but might have to make adjustments to use a higher biodiesel blend in cooler weather.

[49] Examples of items which require more frequent inspection include emergency push-out windows, emergency doors, emergency safety marking lights, brake systems, and wheelchair lift and restraint systems (Schiavone 2010). A complete list of items is available at the Electronic Code of Federal Regulations Website: Electronic Code of Federal Regulations. 2011. Title 49 – Transportation, Subtitle B – Other Regulations Relating to Transportation. Accessed 11 May 2011: http://ecfr.gpoaccess.gov/cgi/t/text/text-idx?c=ecfr&tpl=/ecfrbrowse/Title49/49cfrv2_02.tpl.

[50]The maintenance intervals are for guidance purposes only. A vehicle's specific maintenance manual will have more detailed information about maintenance intervals. The schedule is available at the following website:
http://cumminsengines.com/sites/every/applications/urban_bus_shuttle/EPA_2010_ISB67_Urban.page?section=maintenance

Table 17 - Cummins 6.7L Maintenance Intervals

Maintenance Item	Hours	Months
Oil and Filter[51]	500	6
Primary Fuel Filter[52]	500	6
Secondary Fuel Filter	500	6
Overhead Adjustment	5,000	48
Standard Coolant Change[53]	2,000	24
Coalescing Filter	2,500	
DEF Filter	6,500	
Particulate Filter Cleaning	6,500	

Note: If engine is equipped with an optional coolant filter, it will need replacement at the same intervals as the oil filters

Staff should establish regular PM checklists and schedules from the criteria and recommendations above and should continually monitor the performance and effectiveness of the PM protocol. Such monitoring will allow the Refuge to develop a tailored PM schedule for the Refuge that incorporates local operating conditions and past experience. Staff can then adjust the service schedule if the manufacturer's recommended intervals are inappropriate.

Due to anticipated service along the unpaved portion of Refuge Road (south of lot 4), the Refuge may wish to incorporate more frequent inspection of tire wear, undercarriage components and body wear into their PM planning. Gravel roads may cause additional wear-and-tear on vehicles, but this should not be a major concern for the Refuge, given the low total mileage planned for the unpaved roads sections.

Vehicle Purchase Considerations

Used Vehicle Options

The Refuge requested that the vehicle selection analysis explore used vehicle options as a means of reducing the costs of vehicle purchase. The FAR stipulates the GSA as the sole source for vehicle purchasing for all federal agencies, but the GSA Autochoice does not list used vehicles.

One option for federal agencies to acquire used vehicles from other federal agencies is the GSAXcess interface. GSAXcess is a web platform that allows federal agencies and other authorized users to access the Federal Disposal System. Federal agencies can report excess property or search for the excess property reported by other federal agencies. GSAXcess lists a range of property types, including vehicles, computer equipment, and lab equipment. Federal agencies interested in an excess property would select the item in GSAXcess, at which point GSA evaluates the eligibility and priority of the requesting agency and facilitates the transfer and approval process. The web platform also features a "Want List" feature that allows the federal agency user to be notified when property items become available based on selected criteria. FWS has an approving officer for all requests within the agency, and Refuge staff can work with this officer for guidance in making property requests through GSAXcess.

---

[51] Assuming normal duty cycle.
[52] OEM-Supplied; intervals may vary.
[53] Extended coolant drain/flush/fill intervals may be followed when certain requirements are met.

There are several benefits and drawbacks to acquiring a used vehicle through GSAXcess and the Federal Disposal System. The benefits include significant cost savings, environmental benefits of purchasing an existing vehicle, and a structured acquisition structure through GSA. However, GSAXcess has limited vehicle availability; GSAXcess had no transit vehicles in the 20 to 30 passenger range available as of the date of publication. The non-transit vehicles listed on GSAXcess are often damaged, require extensive maintenance or repair, and/or are located thousands of miles from the Refuge. Therefore, GSAXcess may be a feasible option, subject to vehicle availability, but the Refuge should carefully weigh the costs of maintenance and acquisition of any vehicles available through GSAXcess. The analysis recommends that Refuge staff register with the "Want List" feature of GSAXcess and work with the FWS approving officer to monitor the possibility of a used vehicle purchase through the Federal Disposal System.

In special circumstances, the GSA may grant a waiver to an agency seeking to purchase a vehicle elsewhere. However, since new vehicles that would meet the Refuge's needs are available for purchase on the GSA schedule, the Refuge does not have a strong case for a waiver. While there are used vehicles that would generally meet Refuge requirements, the Refuge would not likely succeed in receiving a waiver to purchase these vehicles. Due to the small selection of vehicles available on GSAXcess and the difficulty of obtaining a GSA waiver, the project team recommends that the Refuge look to purchase a new vehicle from the 2011 GSA schedule, such as the vehicles outlined earlier in this section.

Leasing Assessment

The project team explored the possibility of a short-term lease to pilot the use of vehicle for its programs and special events. A short-term lease would potentially allow the Refuge to test the use of a transit vehicle without making the commitment to purchase a vehicle. The following brief investigation into potential leasing options in the region demonstrates that leasing would not be feasible for Parker River.

The Refuge must purchase or lease all vehicles through the GSA, which offers two basic options for leasing vehicles. GSA Fleet offers a long-term lease out of the Hooksett (NH) Fleet Management Center for a 24-passenger bus. However, the minimum term for the lease is 12 years, making this option unfeasible for a short-term test of the transit concept. The cost of a long-term lease is $633 per month plus $0.58 per mile. The GSA also offers a Short-Term Rental (STR) program through which federal agencies can lease vehicles on 60-day contracts through a local, private rental agency. Federal agencies bid on a vehicle and then receive a rental price, which agencies can decline if it exceeds their budget or needs. The GSA sets cost ceilings on short-term rentals, though these ceilings often far exceed the actual rental price. The largest vehicle available through the STR program is a 15-passenger van, with a cost ceiling of $2,400 to $2,800 per month. The renting agency can renew STR contracts in 60-day increments.[54]

Parker River may consider submitting a bid on a 15-passenger van to test the use of a designated vehicle for interpretive and educational programs. However, the STR program can be costly, and Refuge staff should only engage in a short-term rental if the benefits exceed the costs. If the Refuge pursues this option, staff should set a budgetary limit in advance, based on the perceived value to refuge programs, partners, and congestion relief. Staff should then decline the bid if it exceeds the budgeted amount.

A vehicle lease arrangement gives the Refuge the advantage of testing the use of a transit vehicle prior to making a purchase. Feedback gathered during a leasing period could inform the vehicle purchase and future service planning. However, in the case of Parker River, leasing is significantly more expensive over the long term than vehicle purchase. The type of vehicle that would best meet the Refuge's estimated

---

[54] GSA Concord Fleet Management Center. 31 March 2011. Personal conversation.

program needs is not available for lease, and the 15-passenger van that may be available through the STR program may not be appropriate for a pilot program because of the small passenger capacity. Therefore, this transit analysis will not further consider leasing as a viable option, focusing instead on the vehicle purchase option.

Vehicle Assessment Conclusions

The vehicle selection analysis in this report has established a sufficient passenger capacity, general specification, optional equipment list, and fuel type for a vehicle to meet the Refuge's needs. A 28-passenger light-duty shuttle bus will meet the Refuge's basic needs at the lowest capital cost. A medium-duty shuttle bus can also meet the Refuge's needs and offer service with higher mileage routes and with more taxing physical conditions, such as steep grades or heavy traffic. Both types of vehicles should include the following options:[55]

- Engine block heater
- Heated fuel-water separator
- Tinted and tempered passenger windows
- LED exterior lighting
- Daytime running lights
- Public address system
- Energy saving interior lighting
- Tilt steering wheel
- One piece vinyl transit grade flooring
- Padded woven fabric surface walls
- Padded woven fabric surface ceiling
- Track-mounted seating
- Fabric woven grey cloth seat covering (vinyl on basic)
- Air + Spring Suspension (air adjustable suspension)
- Custom color paint
- Overhead parcel racks
- Wheelchair lift
- Wheelchair occupant restraint system

Such a vehicle would be capable of serving the Refuge's primary needs of environmental education and interpretive programs and special events, as well as offering a potential service for peak visitation periods.

To procure a new vehicle as specified above, the Refuge will need additional funding. Staff should examine the available equipment list and vehicle options carefully in order to acquire a vehicle most tailored to their needs and goals. A modern diesel engine will allow for the use of biodiesel in a light blend (B20 or less) without any modifications and would enable the Refuge to fuel the vehicle from the existing fuel tanks at the Refuge headquarters. The Refuge could accommodate some light maintenance and inspections for the vehicles described in this analysis within its current facilities and staff capacity and refer the vehicle to local service providers for major and scheduled servicing along with PM work.

This analysis suggests that a light-duty "standard" option, 28-passenger, diesel-powered bus with options such as overhead parcel racks, custom paint and wheelchair lift and restraints in addition to the standard

---

[55] The heated fuel-water separator may not be available for light-duty vehicles. While this feature would be useful for winter driving, it is not necessary for safe vehicle operation.

options (included in the GSA schedule vehicles noted above) would offer the best combination of value, practicality, and ease of operation. The Refuge may also consider adding a hybrid-drive option to the vehicle, which would increase the purchase price by approximately $40,000 or $50,000 but would demonstrate environmental leadership and offer modest fuel savings.

The anticipated mileage of 4,500-5,500 miles per year combined with the relatively low site-specific impacts will allow for the development of a relatively simple PM schedule. An annual service combined with limited in-season services and regular safety inspections will likely meet most specified service interval requirements. A PM program should examine these requirements and schedule inspections on-site when possible and utilize outside facilities as needed.

SECTION 5: UTILIZATION ANALYSIS

The Refuge's existing conditions and visitation patterns demonstrate a need for a transit vehicle, and the GSA schedule offers several vehicles that could meet the Refuge's needs. The next step to determine feasibility for a transit vehicle at the Refuge is a utilization analysis. The utilization analysis includes the broad categories of vehicle use and how these uses relate to Refuge priorities. It also includes the delineation of routes where the vehicle would offer service, which will help better define the vehicle's anticipated mileage and fuel use. Finally, this section contains a scheduling analysis to identify when the vehicle will be used as well as time periods that offer opportunities for new uses.

> **Defining Environmental Education and Interpretive Programs**
>
> FWS defines environmental education and interpretation as two distinct wildlife-dependent recreational uses for the National Wildlife Refuge System.[1] Refuge staff at Parker River NWR also distinguish between environmental education and interpretation in planning for future programming. However, the way that Refuge staff would utilize a transit vehicle for both types of programs would be very similar, for purposes of this analysis. Both types of programs would have similar types of routes, mileage, and occupancy. The primary difference is that Refuge staff would anticipate using a transit vehicle for approximately 90 percent of environmental education programs, but for only 50 percent of interpretation programs. The Transit Planning Study treats the use of a transit vehicle for both types of programs as one category, considering that actual programming will be distinct between those programs and that the utilization rates for the vehicle will differ.

Vehicle Uses

The project team examined two broad uses for the transit vehicle: programs and special events as a primary use and a shuttle option as a secondary use. The Refuge's Transit Planning Study goals (see Table 1) inform how the Refuge should utilize a transit vehicle and make decisions regarding scheduling conflicts for the vehicle. The goals prioritize environmental education and interpretive programs; congestion relief, especially during special events; environmental leadership; and engagement of partners for programs and events. The project team also analyzed specific categories of uses, with prioritization of uses to inform vehicle scheduling. The Transit Planning Study treats environmental education and interpretive programs similarly, although the FWS considers these as distinct recreational uses; the sidebar "Defining Environmental Education and Interpretive Programs" explains the consideration of these programs.

Goals

The use of a transit vehicle for programs and special events would directly help the Refuge meet the following Transit Feasibility Study goals:

1. Expand visitor opportunities for interpretation and environmental education
2. Reduce congestion and enhance visitor experience during festivals and special events
3. Engage partners to enhance environmental education opportunities

The Refuge could also reduce vehicular congestion, increase safety, and reduce impacts to species through removing some of the private vehicles currently associated with programs and special events. Finally, the Refuge would demonstrate environmental leadership in transportation related to interpretation and environmental education through the reduction of fuel use associated with these programs.

As a secondary use for the transit vehicle, during times that no programs or special events are scheduled, the Refuge could run the vehicle between destinations in Newburyport and on the Refuge. This shuttle option would allow visitors to access the Refuge without the use of a personal vehicle. The use of a transit vehicle for transportation between Newburyport and Refuge destinations would directly help address the following Transit Feasibility Study goals:

1. Reduce congestion on the Refuge
2. Engage partners to enhance environmental education opportunities and leverage funding and capacity for vehicle operation and management
3. Expand visitor opportunities for interpretation and environmental education
4. Demonstrate environmental leadership in transportation

The shuttle option would only address congestion and environmental goals if it displaced some of the visitors who currently use personal vehicles with visitors who accessed the Refuge via transit. Also, since the shuttle transportation would likely incorporate tours led by Refuge staff, the shuttle would also allow the Refuge to reach new audiences for interpretation and environmental education. The Refuge could also allow its partners to use the transit vehicle for shuttling visitors during special events.

Use Prioritization

The project team assigned potential uses of a transit vehicle into several specific categories based upon type of activity and the agency or actor responsible for the activity. The team then ranked the use categories in order of priority relative to the Refuge's vehicle use goals. Table 18 summarizes the categories of uses and priorities for each.

Table 18: Categories of Uses and Priorities

Category	Description	Priority
Refuge-led Programs	Environmental education and interpretive programs led by Refuge staff	High
Refuge-led Events	Special events led and/or sponsored by the Refuge (may include participation or co-sponsorship by refuge partners)	High
Partner-led Programs	Education and interpretive programs, led by refuge partners, that take place on the Refuge	Medium
Local and Regional Special Events	Special events in Newburyport and surrounding areas (with various sponsors) during which the Refuge could offer tours	Medium
Group Educational Trips	Guided educational programs for school or senior groups, focused on underserved populations	Medium, or as scheduling permits
Shuttle Option	Shuttle between Newburyport commuter rail station, downtown, and the Refuge; to be combined with staff-led interpretive program	As scheduling permits
Partner-led Programs for Target Groups	Programs targeted at underserved populations (e.g. low-income senior housing, urban schools, Boys and Girls Club, and Lowell Association for the Blind)	As scheduling permits

The highest-priority use for the transit vehicle would be for Refuge-led programs and events. Refuge staff discussed several ideas for environmental and interpretive education programs that are either in development stages or could be instituted if the Refuge owned a transit vehicle. The Refuge intends to focus new program content on refuge management and is developing a "marquee" program, which would highlight cultural history, natural history, and management practices through a Refuge tour. The Refuge also would like to expand access to visitors for guided interpretation activities during times when refuge parking lots are closed due to the presence of piping plovers or high visitation. For example, the Refuge could offer one tour per day during the summer that would take participants to wildlife viewing areas even when parking lots are full. The use of a Refuge vehicle for such a tour would discourage non-participants from parking at these closed lots. Finally, unlike Mass Audubon, which offers numerous fee-based programs on the Refuge, FWS staff can offer programs free of charge. Refuge staff also have more flexibility in using areas of the Refuge typically closed to the public and including wildlife management strategies as part of their programs.

The priority rankings in Table 18 can provide guidance for assigning the vehicle to specific activities, as outlined in the next section on scheduling. The Refuge should first use the transit vehicle for its own programs, festivals, and special events. Second, the Refuge should allow Mass Audubon to use the vehicle for Wednesday morning birding programs that take place on the Refuge. Third, the Refuge should use the vehicle to expand its educational and interpretive program offerings in several ways. The Refuge can offer tours, originating in downtown Newburyport, in association with existing City-sponsored festivals. Also, the Refuge can offer transportation and tours to student and senior groups, particularly those from underserved communities that cannot afford their own transportation.

Once the Refuge has scheduled the transit vehicle for the highest-priority activities, staff can consider other uses that would help its partners to meet their goals. During times when the Refuge is not using the vehicle for its own programs (including programs that will be developed and expanded in future years), Mass Audubon may possibly use the vehicle for programs other than Wednesday morning birding originating out of Joppa Flats. Finally, during weekend days when the transit vehicle is not otherwise in use, the Refuge can use the vehicle to bring visitors from the Newburyport commuter rail station to the Refuge. This use would be structured to align with Refuge goals and minimize impacts associated with increased visitation.

Routes

The analysis of transit vehicle routes considers that the Refuge and its partners will primarily occupy a single transit vehicle for environmental education and interpretive programs and special events. During times when programs and events are not scheduled, the Refuge may consider a secondary use of the vehicle for shuttling visitors between key destinations around the Refuge and the City of Newburyport, likely in conjunction with structured Refuge programming. The following section details the two types of routes on which a transit vehicle would operate.

Program and Special Event Uses and Routes

Routes for most programs and special events would originate at the Refuge Headquarters or the Joppa Flats Education Center, as these locations offer a convenient meeting and orientation point. The routes would include one or more stops within the Refuge and then return to the origin. Some transit vehicle trips associated with special events and festivals would originate in downtown Newburyport and may or may not stop at the Refuge Headquarters on the way to the Refuge. Table 19 shows the primary origins and destinations for transit vehicle use, as well as the mileage, headway time, and approximate fuel usage for each segment.[56] The transit vehicle may serve other destinations, including other points for interpretation and education within the Refuge. These points are guides to approximate distance and visualize typical usage patterns. Note that the Refuge Headquarters is located adjacent to the Joppa Flats Education Center. The mileage between Joppa Flats and destinations on the Refuge is equivalent to the mileage from the Headquarters.

Table 19: Mileage for Segments of Transit Vehicle Trips

Segment	Mileage	Time (Minutes)	Fuel Use
HQ to Lot 1	2.5 miles	7	0.4 gal
Lot 1 to Hellcat/Lot 4	3.5 miles	10	0.5-0.6 gal
Hellcat to Stage Island/Lot 7	2.1 miles	6	0.3-0.4 gal
Newburyport to HQ	1.5 miles	5	0.2-0.3 gal

The exact route and mileage for each program would vary depending upon program type and purpose. However, due to the layout of the Refuge's transportation infrastructure, all programs taking place on the Refuge would have an out-and-back pattern. The round trip mileage and time for several potential program routes are listed in Table 20. Each route is listed by its origin and southernmost destination on Plum Island; because Refuge Road has no "spur" roads, the program may include multiple stops on the Refuge prior to reaching the listed destination without increasing the total mileage of the trip. Figure 24 graphically depicts the location of several key destinations on the refuge.

Table 20: Total Mileage for Transit Vehicle Routes

Route	Mileage	Travel Time (Minutes)	Fuel Use
HQ to Lot 1	5 miles	14	0.8-0.9 gal
HQ to Hellcat/Lot 4	12 miles	34	1.8-2.1 gal
HQ to Stage Island/Lot 7	16.2 miles	42	2.5-2.8 gal
Newburyport to Lot 1	8 miles	24	1.2-1.4 gal
Newburyport to Hellcat/Lot 4	15 miles	44	2.3-2.6 gal
Newburyport to Stage Island/Lot 7	19.2 miles	52	2.9-3.3 gal

---

[56] Shuttle fuel use is estimated using a range of 5.8 mpg for medium-duty vehicles and 6.6 mpg for light-duty vehicles. In some cases, the total fuel uses for both types of vehicles are the same due to rounding. These numbers are estimates for planning purposes only. The actual fuel use will vary based on driver behavior, idling, road conditions, and other factors.

Figure 24: Trip Destinations for Programs and Special Events

Destinations for Programs and Special Events
1: Refuge Headquarters
2: Lot 1 and Visitor Contact Station
3: Hellcat Wildlife Observation Area
4: Stage Island Pool

Refuge and Mass Audubon staff schedule most of their programs to last between two and three hours. Therefore, most programs may include an additional one to two hours of education and interpretation activities, outside of travel time, both in and out of the vehicle. The transit vehicle enhances this time by allowing Refuge and Audubon staff to answer questions or interact with participants during travel time as well. Also, due to the longer travel time to reach the southernmost destinations of the Refuge, the Refuge may choose shorter program routes for times with scheduling conflicts or younger children with shorter attention spans.

The Refuge occasionally closes Refuge Road south of the Hellcat Wildlife Observation Area, due to weather conditions. When the road is closed, generally for several weeks during the winter, programs will only include destinations accessible by the open segments of Refuge Road.

The routes described in Tables 19 and 20 and illustrated in Figure 24 compose the majority of existing and future refuge programs and events, but some programs and events may deviate from these routes. For example, the Merrimack River Eagle Festival, held in February, includes sites around Newburyport, Amesbury, and Salisbury (see Figure 25), but it does not include sites within the Refuge boundaries. As the Refuge expands its tour offerings in conjunction with special events in the area, the routes may also include some deviation from those described above.

Figure 25: Merrimack River Eagle Festival Map

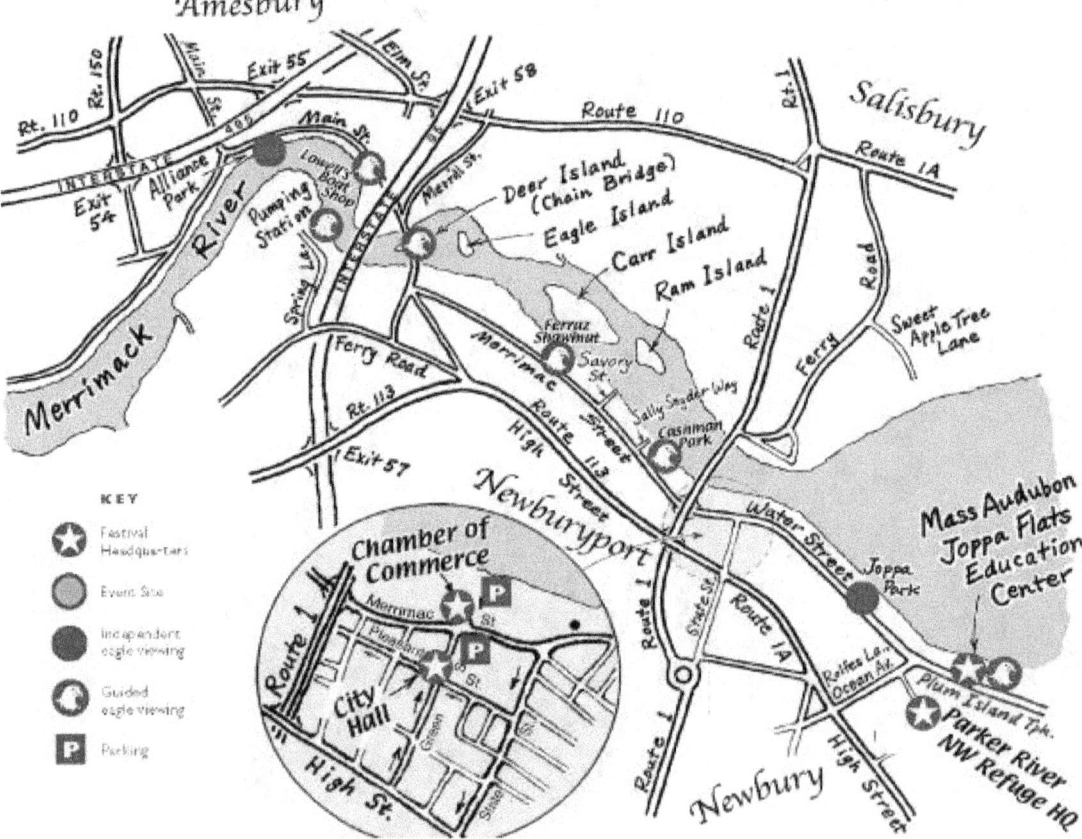

Shuttle Option Routes

The routes for the shuttle option would include transportation to and from nearby mass transit as well as stops in downtown Newburyport to allow visitors to patronize local businesses. The route would originate at the Refuge headquarters, travel to the MBTA commuter rail station in Newburyport, return with visitors to the Refuge headquarters, complete a circuit on the Refuge, drop visitors in downtown Newburyport, drive visitors from downtown to the commuter rail station, and return to the Refuge headquarters. The transit vehicle may either remain in Newburyport during visitor free time or return to the Refuge, based on parking and staff availability. Appendix B contains details and analysis about the use of a shuttle service for the transit vehicle.

Figure 26 shows the key destinations and roads that the transit vehicle would use to shuttle visitors. Table 21 then shows the mileage and travel time for each segment. While the total mileage and travel time are relatively low, the schedules (listed in Appendix B) include buffers to account for loading times, local traffic conditions, and schedule fluctuations. The total duration of shuttle routes and programs would be between four and six hours (see specific options in Appendix B).

Figure 26 – Destinations and Routes for Shuttling Option

Table 21 - Total Mileage and Travel Time for Newburyport Route

Arriving Route	Mileage	Travel Time (Minutes)	Fuel Use
HQ to MBTA Commuter Rail	2.6	8	0.4 gal
MBTA commuter rail to HQ	2.6	8	0.4 gal

Refuge Tour Route	Mileage	Travel Time (Minutes)	Fuel Use
HQ to Stage Island & Return	16.2 miles	42	2.5-2.8 gal

Departing Route	Mileage	Travel Time (Minutes)	Fuel Use
HQ to downtown Newburyport	2.2	5	0.3-0.4 gal
Newburyport to MBTA	1.3	3	0.2 gal
MBTA to HQ	2.6	8	0.4 gal

Total Route	Total Mileage	Total Travel Time (Minutes)	Fuel Use
Refuge and Newburyport Service	27.5	74	4.2-4.7 gal

Note: Travel time does not include time waiting, stopped, or for interpretation and wildlife observation.

Scheduling a Transit Vehicle

The scheduling analysis documents the anticipated uses for a transit vehicle through modeling existing and potential use events for calendar year 2011. Appendix A shows a 12 month calendar with periods of utilization for a 28-passenger transit vehicle. The scheduling analysis shows that the Refuge and its partners would use the transit vehicle for high-priority activities throughout the year. Even during the lowest-visitation months, the project team identified at least two events per week that would utilize the vehicle. During high visitation months, the Refuge would use the vehicle for as many as 25 activities, with multiple events on some days. As expected, the periods with the greatest demand for vehicle use are Saturdays during spring, summer, and fall. Wednesdays are also high-use days due to Mass Audubon's morning and evening birding programs and the Gulf of Maine Institute/Newburyport High School field trips. The months of May through October have the most activities, with the winter months having the fewest.

Mondays, Tuesdays, and Fridays are the days with the least scheduled vehicle utilization, with the exception of Friday morning birding programs, held only during the month of May. Also, while the Refuge and its partners have many events scheduled on Saturdays, the vehicle would have very few activities scheduled for Sundays. The exceptions are a few special events, mostly during August. The weekend vacancy presents opportunities for expanded programmatic offerings or other vehicle uses.

Utilization Conflicts

During the highest-use periods, the calendar shows several periods of conflicting uses. The Refuge should use the prioritization of use categories, as delineated in Table 18, to determine vehicle scheduling during periods of conflicts. In most cases, these conflicts occur on Wednesdays and Saturdays during times that Mass Audubon has regularly-scheduled birding programs. These conflicts include Refuge-led programs such as the monthly Master Naturalist program or the week-long Nature Photography Camp and Refuge Academy. The Refuge-led program would always take precedence over the Audubon-led program. However, the Refuge staff has expressed the desire to let Mass Audubon use the transit vehicle for all of its Wednesday morning birding programs occurring on the Refuge, whereas Mass Audubon would only use the vehicle for other programs if no conflicts with Refuge-led programs existed or Refuge staff granted permission for extenuating circumstances.

The calendar also shows several instances in which Refuge-led programs conflict with scheduled special events, such as Go Fish or the Essex Natural Heritage Area's Trails & Sails. In these cases, the Refuge could reschedule interpretive programs for non-conflicting dates or expand the audience of its programs to include participants from the concurrent festival. Refuge staff would need to make a determination, on a case-by-case basis, as to whether to use a transit vehicle for a regional festival or a regularly-scheduled Mass Audubon birding program. While the Refuge staff would have to carefully plan in advance for the vehicle's use during these high-demand periods, the scheduling conflicts would likely be easy to manage due to the Refuge's close working relationships with its partners.

Opportunities for New Uses

Periods of vehicle inactivity offer opportunities for new programming and activities, led by both the Refuge and its partners; new environmental education and interpretive programs would fulfill the Refuge's goals of enhanced and expanded programming.

Weekdays without regularly-scheduled activities would be optimal for educational programs with student and senior groups. The calendar in Appendix A includes two days per month (one Tuesday and one Friday) allotted for these educational programs. The Refuge could reach out to targeted student groups from local schools during the school year, and to senior groups and youth organizations in underserved communities year-round, to attend programs during these dates. The Refuge would need to invest time in the initial outreach and preparation associated with planning these group programs. If successful, the Refuge could then expand to offer weekday group programs on a more regular basis during other periods of vehicle activity.

Sundays would be a good time for the Refuge to expand its programming in adult education or interpretation for families. The Refuge has scheduled most of its interpretive programs for the general public on Saturdays, and it may consider alternating with Sundays to avoid vehicle use conflicts and also reach a new audience.

During Sundays when the vehicle is not utilized for scheduled activities, the Refuge may consider offering a shuttle option, as described in Appendix B. Such a use could potentially allow more visitors to access the Refuge during high visitation periods, but they would do so within a structured program led by Refuge staff so as not to increase negative impacts to refuge resources.

Utilization Summary

A transit vehicle would provide a significant tool for the Refuge to expand and enhance its current program and special event offerings. The Refuge could find activities for a transit vehicle with relative regularity throughout the year, utilizing the vehicle for programs and events run by the Refuge and its partner agencies. The Refuge would generally operate the vehicle on approximately 10 miles of roads between Newburyport and Plum Island, with occasional routes to other regional destinations. Operating within a limited geographic area and focused on serving program needs, the vehicle would have a relatively low annual VMT and fuel consumption, which would also reduce the annual operating expenses.

The scheduling analysis determines that the Refuge and its partners would not fully utilize the vehicle seven days a week, and they would use the vehicle less frequently during the winter months. The periods of inactivity for the vehicle offer opportunities for the Refuge to expand its environmental education and interpretive programming, to offer programs in conjunction with other local and regional events, and to explore the use of a shuttle service to bring new types of visitors to the Refuge.

If the Refuge chooses to proceed with the acquisition of a transit vehicle, it should aim to utilize the vehicle as frequently as possible and enlist partners to utilize the vehicle for programs that support the Refuge's mission. Greater use of the vehicle would increase the benefits to the Refuge in terms of visitor experience, environmental impacts, and congestion relief, and the Refuge would want to maximize those benefits relative to their investment in the vehicle. However, Refuge staff must also recognize challenges connected with the management and operation of a transit vehicle, such as staff capacity needs and unexpected maintenance issues.

SECTION 6: BUDGET

The previous analysis demonstrates that a transit vehicle could significantly help the Refuge to achieve its goals in the areas of environmental education and interpretive programs, congestion relief, environmental leadership, and partnership expansion. The next step is to ensure the financial feasibility of purchasing and operating a transit vehicle. The brief budget analysis in this section outlines capital expenses, operations and maintenance costs, and potential funding sources. This section does not offer a comprehensive financial plan for a transit vehicle but rather provides basic data, projections, and guidance to assess overall feasibility and help the Refuge plan and budget for a transit vehicle.

Capital Expenses

The total capital expenses of the transit vehicles analyzed in this study, including a five percent addition for acquisition cost through GSA, is included in Table 22.

Table 22: Capital Costs

Item	Expense
Light-Duty Vehicle Base Price	
• Glaval Entourage F550	• $88,624
• Startrans Senator HD	• $92,799
• ChampBus Challenger F550	• $94,695
Light-Duty Vehicle with 5% Acquisition Costs	
• Glaval Entourage F550	• $93,055
• Startrans Senator HD	• $97,439
• ChampBus Challenger F550	• $99,430
Medium-Duty Base Price	
• Glaval Concord II	• $116,621
• Startrans Tourliner	• $132,017
• IC Bus HC	• $134,906
• Turtle Top Odyssey XL	• $142,584
Medium-Duty Vehicle with 5% Acquisition Costs	
• Glaval Concord II	• $122,452
• Startrans Tourliner	• $138,618
• IC Bus HC	• $141,651
• Turtle Top Odyssey XL	• $149,713

Source: GSA Autochoice 2011

The Refuge received $122,300 in FY 2009 from the TRIP grant program. The grant was to be used for the purchase of a 24-passenger, light-duty shuttle bus. Of that amount, approximately $80,000 remains to be used for vehicle purchase.

The Refuge would need $13,100 to cover the capital expenses of purchasing the least-expensive light-duty GSA model, the Glaval Entourage, or $43,000 to cover the cost of the least-expensive medium-duty model, the Glaval Concord II. One funding source for the purchase of a transit vehicle could be a second application to the Sarbanes TRIP program.[57] The Refuge could enhance an application through the evidence presented in this Transit Feasibility Study to better justify and quantify the need for a transit vehicle. Up to ten percent of additional funds could be reserved for contingency and acquisition costs.

The Refuge also may pursue discretionary transportation funding from FWS Region 5. The Refuge should include the purchase of a transit vehicle and the objective of expanded environmental education and interpretive programming in its CCP to emphasize the importance of the vehicle to the Refuge over the next several decades.

Operation and Maintenance Expenses

The primary expenses to operate, manage, and maintain a 28-passenger transit vehicle are included in Table 23.

Table 23: Annual Operations and Maintenance Costs

Item	Annual Expense
CDL license	**$40 per license $100 for shared training materials**
Fuel	**$3,200 – $4,300**
PM Inspections	**$750 - $940 (Labor Only)**
Major service: Anticipate one-two major services per year. Not all costs included would be duplicated.	**$600-$750 (Engine Related)** **$520-$625 (Cab, Body, Accessories, Hydraulic Systems, etc) $350-$440 (Braking System)** **$195-$250 (HVAC Systems)** **$175-$220 (Transmission)** **$75-$100 (Air, General)** **$75-$100 (Frame, Steering)** **$75-$100 (Tires, misc)** $2,000 - $2,600 Total Annual Service Cost (Estimated)[58]
Insurance	**Not needed based on FWS ownership; Mass Audubon has their own insurance**

The total operations and maintenance expenses for a transit vehicle would cost approximately $6,000 to $7,900 per year. The total includes annual fuel cost, cost of CDL licenses, annual PM inspection costs, and total annual service costs (using an average maintenance cost of $0.50 per mile).[59]

The largest annual expense will be for fuel. The estimate of $3,200 to $4,300 per year is calculated on the basis of an annual VMT of 5,000 to 6,250 and an average fuel economy of six miles per gallon. Table 24 shows the range of fuel prices, estimated using local fuel prices on May 13, 2011.[60] Higher blends of biodiesel are slightly more expensive than ULSD, in that each additional five percent of biofuel materials added to conventional diesel raises the price per gallon by approximately $0.07.

---

[57] The Refuge applied to the TRIP program for an additional $80,000 in FY 2011. The application, which was submitted prior to the completion of this Transit Planning Study, would cover the additional capital expenses of a transit vehicle and included funds for acquisition and contingency. The total funding of approximately $160,000 would cover the cost of any of the four transit vehicles analyzed in this study as well as some vehicles with greater passenger capacity.

[58] Johnson, Caley. 2010. Business Case for Compressed Natural Gas in Municipal Fleets. National Renewable Energy Laboratory Technical Report NREL/TP-7A2-47919. Accessed 23 May 2011: http://www.afdc.energy.gov/afdc/pdfs/47919.pdf.

[59] The estimate of $0.50 per mile was identified as an industry standard rate for ULSD maintenance costs in a National Renewable Energy Laboratory report entitled "Business Case for Compressed Natural Gas in Municipal Fleets," published in June of 2010.

[60] Conversation with Mark Pinnenchi of Dennis K. Burke Inc. in Chelsea, MA (current fuel provider for the Refuge), May 13, 2011.

Table 24: Fuel Cost Estimation

Base Price for Diesel	$ 3.84		
Additional Cost for Each 5% of Biofuel	**$ 0.07**		
Cost for B5 Blend	$ 3.91		
Cost for B20 Blend	$ 4.12		
Miles per Gallon	**6**		
Miles per Year	**5,000**		**6,250**
Total Cost			
Diesel	**$ 3,200**	**$ 4,000**	
B5 Blend	**$ 3,258**	**$ 4,073**	
B20 Blend	**$ 3,433**	**$ 4,292**	

Source: Dennis K. Burke, Inc. and Volpe Center estimates

Although fuel costs are difficult to predict, this analysis assumes that fuel costs will rise at a rate of five percent per year. The rising fuel costs combined with an anticipated increase in VMT due to expanded vehicle use will result in significant increases in fuel-related costs over a ten-year lifecycle. For example, if the vehicle were to realize 15,000 miles of use with fuel costs increases of five percent by year 10, the annual fuel cost would be between $15,000 and $16,000.[61] The anticipated VMT is not expected to reach such levels, but it is presented as an example so that the Refuge may anticipate aggressive increases in VMT and fuel cost over 10 years. Table 25 indicates rates of increase in fuel cost over 10 years (using ULSD as an example), and illustrates the dramatic impact fuel cost will have on the costs of operating a vehicle.

Table 25 - Fuel Cost Increase, Various Rates Over 10 Years

Year	\% Annual Increase		
	3%	**5%**	**8%**
1	$3.84	$3.84	$3.84
2	$3.96	$4.03	$4.15
3	$4.07	$4.23	$4.48
4	$4.20	$4.45	$4.84
5	$4.32	$4.67	$5.22
6	$4.45	$4.90	$5.64
7	$4.59	$5.15	$6.09
8	$4.72	$5.40	$6.58
9	$4.86	$5.67	$7.11
10	$5.01	$5.96	$7.68

The total maintenance cost is estimated at $2,750 to $3,540 per year. The annual maintenance costs will remain low over the first years of vehicle use and level out as maintenance items reach their replacement or service intervals. Consistent PM inspections and thorough maintenance will both prolong the vehicle's useful life and ensure efficient operation, both of which will help the Refuge maintain control over annual

---

[61] The calculation is based on a diesel price of $5.96 per gallon, a B5 blend price of $6.07 per gallon, and a B20 blend price of $6 39 per gallon.

operations and maintenance costs. The maintenance cost includes $750 to $940 of labor costs for annual or semi-annual PM inspections, for which some service items may be completed on-site at the Refuge headquarters, thus lowering the total cost. The cost also includes major service items, which are listed in Table 23. Refuge staff will not need to perform major service each year, but rather they should plan for a total yearly budget that can "roll over" to account for more costly but infrequent service needs. The total annual service cost of $2,000 to $2,600 uses a per-mile rate that aggregates major service costs over the life of the vehicle. The estimate is based upon costs from similar types of vehicles, considering operating conditions. The anticipated duty cycle and relative low-wear-and-tear environment at the Refuge should result in lower maintenance costs compared to transit industry standards. The figures above are calculated conservatively to allow for budgetary planning, contract repair work, and any unanticipated maintenance-related expenses.

The annual operations expenses include the costs to train and pay drivers. First, the Refuge and its partners must pay for CDL licenses for all drivers. The cost to add a CDL endorsement to a Massachusetts driver's license for commercial passenger vehicles is approximately $40, although training may require up to an additional $100 per person. The Refuge and its partners should estimate a total cost of $500 for training and license fees, considering that the Refuge can share training materials.[62]

The Refuge is able to keep their costs down in several ways. First, the Refuge plans to use its staff and volunteers as drivers for most programs and events. Second, the transit vehicle will use less fuel and have less wear-and-tear on the vehicle, due to the low mileage of service routes. Finally, as a federal agency, the FWS will not need to pay separate insurance fees for vehicle use.

The Refuge can rely upon several sources of funding to cover operation and maintenance costs. First, the Refuge can explore user fees for programs that utilize the transit vehicles, such as the Nature Photography Day Camp or the tours for the Eagle Festival. The use of a program fee would place some of the cost burden on program and event participants. The estimate for a feasible user fee is calculated based on both the total operating cost of the vehicle and the participant's willingness to pay. The estimated annual operating cost for the transit vehicle during its first year of operation is $6,000 to $7,900. A very conservative estimate of vehicle passengers generated by Refuge activities alone would be 7,000 participants (based on 50 percent of current Refuge program and event participants using the vehicle). The number of total transit vehicle passengers is likely to be much higher, considering participants in partner programs and events and higher participation rates for Refuge programs. With 7,000 passengers, the total fee per passenger to defray fuel costs would be approximately $1 per person.

While the fees to cover costs are very modest, the Refuge may consider charging slightly higher fees as a standard for all programs and events, which would allow them to waive fees for target populations or programs in accordance with Refuge goals. To approximate the fee that a visitor may be willing to pay for a Refuge program or tour, the project team reviewed the admission prices or program fees for a range of attractions near the Refuge (see Table 26). The most similar types of programs are the birding tours offered at Joppa Flats, which range from $8 to $15 for adults, depending on the length of the program. Most admission fees for education and recreational attractions range from $5 to $15 for adults, with discounts for children and seniors. Based on this information, the Refuge may wish to consider a fee structure such as a standard fee of for environmental education and interpretive activities of $3 for adults and $1 for children, which they may waive during selected events or programs. The fee would help cover fuel and maintenance costs while remaining far lower than other area attractions.

---

[62] The Refuge is a Federal agency and does not need to register vehicles with the Massachusetts Department of Motor Vehicles; therefore, there is no vehicle registration fee.

Table 26: Fees for Nearby Attractions

Attraction	Location	Description	Rate
Mass Audubon Joppa Flats Programs	Newburyport, MA	3-hour birding programs	$10-15 adults
		2-hour birding programs	$8-10 adults $5-7 children
Custom House Maritime Museum	Newburyport, MA	Maritime history, art, and heritage exhibits	$7 adult $5 seniors and students Children under 6 free
Crane Beach and Castle Hill	Ipswich, MA	Beach, sand dunes, salt marsh, and Castle Hill estate	$15-25 per vehicle
		Tour of historic house and grounds	$10 adults Children 8-12 free
Wolf Hollow	Ipswich, MA	Gray wolf habitat with interpretive programs	$7.50 adults $5 seniors and children
Seacoast Science Center	Rye, NH	Science center focusing on the natural sciences	$5 adult $2 children 3-12
Isle of Shoals	Portsmouth, NH	Boat tour and natural and historic interpretation	$15-20 adults $6-15 children
Strawbery Banke Museum	Portsmouth, NH	Living history museum and historic park	$15 adults $10 children 5-17

Note: All prices are advertised on attraction websites as of May 2011

Another potential fee source would be the Refuge's gatehouse entrance fees (either at existing levels or through fee increases) for operations of the transit vehicle. With this option, visitors would pay a premium to drive their personal vehicles in the Refuge rather than participate in a group program.

A second operations and maintenance funding source would be contributions from Refuge partners. The Refuge would like to request contributions from partners to cover operations and maintenance costs. The Refuge would require partner agencies to be responsible for fuel costs used during their programs and events, and they would request more modest contributions to overall maintenance costs, on the basis of total operational hours of vehicle use for partner-led programs and events. Mass Audubon could obtain this fee through program fees. In addition to providing cash assistance, the City of Newburyport could potentially provide in-kind maintenance services through its Department of Public Services – Highway Division.

Many other Refuge "Friends groups" collect funds for operation of transit vehicles. Similarly, the Friends of Parker River National Wildlife Refuge to raise funds to cover some portion of long-term operations and maintenance costs.

Feasibility

The budget analysis indicates that the Refuge could feasibly purchase, operate, and maintain a 28-passenger transit vehicle for primary use in programs and special events. The Refuge already has funds to cover much of the capital cost of the vehicle and can seek additional funds. Since the transit vehicle will be shared with Refuge partners, the Refuge may be able to rely on its partners to play a more significant role in providing ongoing funding. The Refuge can also pursue several potential funding sources independently of its partners. The Refuge's ability to purchase and fund the vehicle will depend on availability of outside funding sources, fluctuations in fuel prices, and cooperation of partners. If the Refuge secures funding for the vehicle purchase, the project team recommends that the Refuge conduct a more thorough budget analysis to plan in detail for operations and maintenance expenses over the first five years.

SECTION 7: EVALUATION FRAMEWORK AND CONCLUSIONS

Evaluation of Vehicle Performance

A transit vehicle would help Parker River National Wildlife Refuge expand its program and special event offerings, improve visitors' experiences during these programs and events, and realize environmental benefits by removing personal vehicles from refuge roads and parking lots. The preceding sections outline uses for the vehicle in accordance with the goals and priorities of the Refuge and its partners. Considering those goals and priorities, the following analysis provides criteria and measures to quantifiably estimate the benefits of a transit vehicle. These measures will also allow the Refuge to track its progress in meeting the study's goals.

Each goal includes two to three evaluation criteria, which are simplified and objective to measure effectiveness of the vehicle at meeting each goal. Each evaluation criteria contains a baseline figure from 2010, where available and applicable. Refuge staff and the project team jointly selected performance targets, aimed at five years after the purchase of a transit vehicle.

The Refuge should use these evaluation criteria as guidelines for growing the demand for and use of a transit vehicle, as well as to manage the use of a transit vehicle in a manner that is aligned with the Refuge's goals. The Refuge should evaluate criteria annually and re-set future targets as needed.

Goal: Expand visitor opportunities for interpretation and environmental education

Evaluation Criteria	Baseline Measure (2010)	Target (5 years)
Number of participants in Refuge-led environmental education programs	5,350	8,000
Number of participants in Refuge-led interpretation programs	5,324	8,000
Number of participants in Partner-led programs	5,317	NA
Total for Refuge-led programs	10,674	16,000
Number of environmental education and interpretation programs offered per year	67	100
Percent of environmental education and interpretation programs with a transit option		
Refuge-led environmental education	5%	90%
Refuge-led interpretation	5%	40%
Partner-led	50%[63]	100% for Wednesday morning birding programs on Refuge and 40% for other programs

---

[63] Approximately 50 percent of participants who visit the Refuge as part of a Mass Audubon program travel on a school bus or other shared vehicle.

The evaluation criteria consider the baseline number of participants in environmental education and interpretation programs, as recorded in the 2010 RAPP, along with the total number of programs that Refuge staff reported offering in 2010. The target growth in program participants is based upon historic growth patterns and Refuge staff expectations for development of new programs. Without a transit vehicle, the baseline percentage of programs with a transit option is approximately five percent, considering that some groups provide their own transit vehicles and the Refuge occasionally rents vehicles for special programs.

By 2015, the Refuge would like to increase program participation to 16,000, an increase of approximately 50 percent, which would accompany an increase in the number of programs the Refuge offers each year (from 67 to 100). The Refuge has not set targets for growth in partner programs, which is outside of their control. The five-year targets reflect the goals of Refuge staff to use the transit vehicle for 90 percent of environmental education programs and 50 percent of interpretation programs that occur on the Refuge. The Refuge also plans to require Mass Audubon to use the transit vehicle for all Wednesday morning birding programs that bring visitors to the Refuge, as well any other Refuge-based programs that do not conflict with existing or new Refuge-led programs.

Goal: Reduce vehicular congestion on the Refuge; reduce vehicular impacts to plant and animal species; increase the safety of visitors and staff; and reduce congestion and enhance visitor experience during festivals and special events.

Evaluation Criteria	Baseline Measure (2010)	Target (5 years)
Estimated VMT associated with Refuge-led environmental education programs	31,208	5,000
Estimated VMT associated with Refuge-led interpretation programs	31,056	22,000
Estimated VMT associated with partner-led programs	16,216	12,516
Number of visitors served by transit during special events	520	1,900

The Refuge goal to reduce vehicular congestion, particularly congestion associated with programs and special events, is expressed through the VMT that results from these programs. The baseline measures are composed primarily of VMT from private vehicles, since only five percent of current Refuge programs use transit vehicles. The target measures for the Refuge are primarily from a transit vehicle, and the target VMT for partner-led programs are a mix of transit and non-transit vehicles. The calculations are based on a series of calculations, Refuge data, and assumptions about current and future program routes. The targets also follow the Refuge's goals for use of the transit vehicle. Ninety percent of environmental education programs would use the transit vehicle, 50 percent of interpretation programs would use the vehicle, 100 percent of Mass Audubon's Wednesday morning birding programs that take place on the Refuge would use the vehicle, and approximately 40 percent of remaining Mass Audubon programs (such as birding certificate programs, photography programs, and school groups) would use the vehicle.[64] If the

---

[64] The baseline VMT for Refuge-led programs is based on the number of participants in environmental education and interpretation programs in the 2010 RAPP, divided by the average vehicle occupancy rate for the Refuge (2.4 persons per vehicle). The project team then multiplied this figure by the estimated average VMT per program (14 miles). To estimate the target for five years after vehicle purchase, the project team calculated an increase in participation in environmental education programs, according to estimates from Table 11: Estimated Growth in Program and Event Participation. Then, the Refuge targeted that 90 percent of environmental program participants would use a transit vehicle instead of their personal vehicle, resulting in a total VMT for these programs of approximately 5,000. The target of 22,000 VMT associated with

Refuge reaches its targets, it would reduce the total VMT associated with its programs from approximately 62,000 to approximately 27,000, a reduction of nearly 60 percent. The Refuge would reduce the VMT associated with all programs, including partner-led programs, from 78,500 to 39,500, a reduction of approximately 50 percent.

Currently, the Refuge serves approximately 520 visitors in transit vehicles during special events (see Table 10). If the Refuge had a transit vehicle to use during all special events, including new events run by partner agencies, the Refuge could serve as many as 2,400 visitors. Refuge staff chose to target 1,900 visitors for transit vehicle use during special events, assuming that the Refuge may not fill the vehicle to capacity during all special events.

Goal: Demonstrate environmental leadership in transportation related to interpretation and environmental education

Evaluation Criteria	Baseline Measure (2010)	Target (5 years after vehicle purchase)
Estimated fuel use associated with Refuge-led programs	2,460 gallons	1,000 gallons
Estimated fuel use associated with partner-led programs	800 gallons	850 gallons
GHG emissions associated with Refuge-led programs	21.9 metric tons of carbon dioxide (CO_2) equivalent	9.5 metric tons of CO_2 equivalent
GHG emissions associated with partner-led programs	7.1 metric tons of CO_2 equivalent	7.6 metric tons of CO_2 equivalent

The baseline estimate of total fuel use associated with Refuge programs is 2,460 gallons, and the estimate for partner-led programs is 800 gallons.[65][66] The baseline fuel use of partner-led programs is 800 gallons. The target fuel use for five years after vehicle purchase is based upon the target VMT for Refuge-led and

---

interpretation programs reflects 50 percent of interpretation programs using the transit vehicles. Note that the total VMT associated with both of these programs combined would be approximately 90,000 miles in 2015 without the use of a transit vehicle.

Mass Audubon calculated that it led 3,591 visitors to the Refuge as part of group programs in 2010, of which 2,693 used their own buses (such as school buses). Mass Audubon recorded an additional 1,726 participants in its public programs on the Refuge, for a total of 2,624 visitors using personal vehicles for transportation during programs. In 2010, the total VMT associated with these participants was 15,306, based on an average vehicle occupancy rate of 2.4 and an average program trip length of 14 miles. Mass Audubon estimates that 65 of their 87 group programs use their own buses, for a total of 910 VMT for these programs in 2010. Therefore the 2010 baseline total for Mass Audubon programs was 16,216.

The calculation of the five-year target VMT for partner-led programs is a bit more complex. First, the Refuge would like to require all Wednesday morning birding programs that take place on the Refuge to use transit vehicles. Mass Audubon estimates that they lead 30 such programs per year to the Refuge. At 14 miles per program, the target VMT for these programs would be 420 miles. Mass Audubon leads an additional 160 public programs to the Refuge each year, of which the Refuge would like to require 40 percent to use the transit vehicle. This would result in 64 programs at 14 miles each, with a total VMT of 896 miles. The remaining 96 programs would have an average of nine participants per program, a vehicle occupancy rate of 2.4 persons per vehicle, and a per-vehicle VMT of 14 miles, resulting in a total VMT of 5,040. Mass Audubon also leads 87 group programs to the Refuge, of which 65 use their own buses for a total of 910 VMT. Mass Audubon notes that approximately 900 people attend group programs not in buses, for a total VMT of 5,250 (based on standard vehicle occupancy and trip length). Therefore, the total VMT associated with all Mass Audubon-led programs on the Refuge is 12,516 (420+896+5,040+910+5,250). This target does not reflect any growth in Mass Audubon program participation.

[65] The baseline estimate for Refuge programs is based on the total VMT associated with Refuge-led programs (62,264) and an average fuel efficiency of American drivers' vehicles of 25.3 miles per gallon (mpg). The estimated baseline fuel use for partner led programs considers a VMT of approximately 15,300 for participants who use their own vehicles, based on the average American fleet fuel efficiency. The estimate also includes the VMT of 910 for group programs that use a transit vehicle, estimating a fuel efficiency of five miles per gallon.
[66] Union of Concerned Scientists. 2007. "Fuel Economy Basics." Clean Vehicles. Accessed 18 May 2011: http://www.ucsusa.org/clean_vehicles/solutions/cleaner_cars_pickups_and_suvs/fuel-economy-basics.html

partner-led programs. The total target fuel use associated with partner-led programs would be 852 gallons.[67] The slight increase in fuel use is due to the relatively small size of public programs and the lower fuel efficiency of transit vehicles compared to personal vehicles. However, with the use of a transit vehicle, Mass Audubon could increase the number of participants served without increasing its fuel use by increasing average program size for public programs. Currently, the average program size is nine people, but the transit vehicle could accommodate up to 18 additional participants per program. The Refuge could also improve the fuel savings by using a hybrid vehicle.

The Refuge could reduce the greenhouse gas emissions associated with its programs by 12.4 metric tons per year. This would be equivalent to removing 2.4 passenger vehicles from the road for a year or to the emissions related to the electricity use of 1.5 American homes.[68] For partner-led programs, the total CO_2 emissions in five years would likely be higher due to growth in program participation, but the use of a transit vehicle would allow the accommodation of more participants with only a modest increase in emissions.

Goal: Engage partners to enhance environmental education opportunities and leverage funding and capacity for vehicle operation and management

Evaluation Criteria	Baseline Measure (2010)	Target (5 years)
VMT to serve partner programs or access partner destinations	16,216	12,516
Percent of vehicle operations, maintenance, and/or capital costs shared by partners	N/A	100% of fuel costs for programs that use transit vehicle and pro-rated cost-sharing for maintenance based on percentage of VMT use of the vehicle

Refuge staff would like to require Mass Audubon to use the transit vehicle for all Wednesday morning programs taking place on the Refuge. The Refuge would also like to make the vehicle available for Mass Audubon for its other programs, but only during times that the Refuge did not need the vehicle for its own activities. The detailed calculation of the five-year VMT target is listed above.

Refuge staff would like its partners to pay for all fuel used during partner-led programs. It would also target some more modest contributions towards vehicle maintenance, based upon the total relative VMT of the Refuge-led programs and the partner-led programs. Additionally, staff from both Mass Audubon and the Refuge would become certified drivers for the vehicle.

---

[67] For the VMT associated with Mass Audubon programs, 2,226 are associated with transit vehicles, which have an estimated fuel efficiency of five mpg for school buses. The total fuel for these vehicles is approximately 445 gallons. The remaining 10,290 miles of their VMT are associated with personal vehicles. Using an average fuel efficiency of 25.3 mpg, the total fuel associated with this VMT would be approximately 407 gallons.

[68] All carbon dioxide equivalent calculations are from the U.S. Environmental Protection Agency's Greenhouse Gas Equivalencies Calculator. The calculator is available at http://www.epa.gov/cleanenergy/energy-resources/calculator.html.

Transit Planning Study Conclusions

The transit planning study considered the Refuge goals and mission, existing conditions, and anticipated future growth to determine the feasibility of a transit vehicle for use in Refuge programs and special events. The project team evaluated current and future visitor demand for a transit vehicle; vehicles available to the Refuge; potential vehicle uses, routes, and schedules; and operations and maintenance management and budget considerations. The study indicates that a 28-passenger transit vehicle could help the Refuge to meet its goals of expanding visitor opportunities for interpretation and environmental education, reducing vehicular congestion on the Refuge, demonstrating environmental leadership in transportation, and engaging partners to enhance environmental education opportunities.

In addition to the primary utility of the transit vehicle for programs and events, the Refuge could occasionally use a vehicle to transport visitors between the City of Newburyport, the Newburyport commuter rail station, and staff-led programs at the Refuge. The Refuge and its partners could also use a vehicle to offer programs to schools and senior groups from nearby urban and underserved areas, many of which cannot currently provide their own transportation to the Refuge. Both of these secondary uses would be based upon vehicle availability and would be designed to conform to the Refuge's mission.

The study found that the ongoing operations and maintenance of a transit vehicle would be financially feasible. The Refuge already has funds to cover much of the capital cost of the vehicle and can seek additional funds. The annual operating and maintenance costs may be collected from user fees and/or contributions from partner organizations.

Key Findings

- The current and planned programs of the Refuge currently account for an estimated 62,265 VMT each year from participants' personal vehicles. Trends of growing participation in these programs since 2006 suggest increased VMT in the future. Partner-led programs and events account for an even greater VMT, demonstrating a strong potential for an alternative transportation solution to reduce VMT related to programs and special events.
- The total initial annual VMT of a transit vehicle would be between 4,500 and 5,500 miles, with anticipated growth of up to 9,600 miles by 2020 (due to expanding program and event participation).
- The purchase and utilization of a 28-passenger shuttle bus is a feasible and recommended strategy to meet the Refuge's basic needs of providing and serving environmental education and interpretive programs and special events, as well as offering a potential service for peak visitation periods. A "standard" option, 28-passenger, diesel-powered bus with options such as overhead parcel racks, custom paint and wheelchair lift and restraints would offer the best combination of value, practicality, and ease of operation.
- GSA offers three light-duty and four medium-duty 28-passenger vehicles that would help enhance Refuge interpretive and environmental education programs and reduce congestion on the Refuge. Outfitted with equipment and features relative to the Refuge's physical conditions and accessibility needs, the costs of the vehicles would be as follows:
  - Light-Duty
    - $88,623.89 – Glaval Entourage F550
    - $92,799.42 – Startrans Senator HD
    - $94,695.47 – ChampBus Challenger F550
  - Medium-Duty
    - $116,620.66 – Glaval Concord II

- $132,017.10 – Startrans Tourliner
- $134,905.70 – IC Bus HC
- $142,583.72 – Turtle Top Odyssey XL

- A modern diesel engine will allow for the use of biodiesel in a light blend (B20 or less) without any modifications and would enable the Refuge to fuel the vehicle from the existing fuel tanks at the Refuge headquarters. The relatively low anticipated mileage of the vehicle would make the purchase of a hybrid vehicle economically infeasible, although the Refuge may choose to purchase a hybrid vehicle to achieve environmental leadership goals.

- If the Refuge and its partners utilized a transit vehicle in place of individual participant vehicles for their programs and special events, they would use the vehicle at least two days per week year-round and during 25 events per month or more during high visitation periods in the spring and summer.

- The Refuge and the project team estimate that 50 percent of off-site interpretation programs and 90 percent of environmental education programs will utilize the transit vehicle. Those utilization rates, combined with anticipated growth in participation, would result in approximate annual VMT reductions of 30,000 miles for interpretation programs and 52,000 miles for environmental education programs by 2020 (see Tables 12 through 14 for approximate VMT reduction impacts of a transit vehicle). The Refuge would reduce its greenhouse gas emissions by approximately 10.5 metric tons of CO_2 equivalent for interpretation programs and 18.3 metric tons of CO_2 equivalent for environmental education programs, based on current and projected VMT and fuel use for environmental education and interpretive program participants.

Recommendations

The Transit Planning Study recommends that the Refuge pursue purchase of a transit vehicle for its environmental education and interpretive programs and special events. The vehicle would have significant impacts in enhancing these programs and events, and it would also have minor impacts in overall congestion relief, environmental leadership, and partnerships.

The Study offers general guidelines that will assist the Refuge staff in managing and operating a transit vehicle. These guidelines pertain to demand estimation, vehicle selection, route planning, scheduling, and budgeting. Using these guidelines as a foundation, the project team recommends that the Refuge staff work with its partners to develop a management plan or select management guidelines for the operation of a transit vehicle.

Specifically, the following recommendations will also enhance the Refuge's ability to manage a transit vehicle:

- A transit vehicle would help the Refuge enhance its environmental education and interpretive programs while alleviating some of the congestion on Refuge roads and parking lots during high-visitation periods. The vehicle should be used primarily for Refuge-led programs and events, and the Refuge could require its partner agencies to utilize the vehicle for selected programs that take place on the Refuge to reduce traffic associated with these programs.

- The Refuge can exercise control over the percentage of programs that use the transit vehicle by requiring program participants to use the transit vehicle instead of their personal automobiles. They can also require partner agencies to do the same for selected programs, on the basis of vehicle availability. Refuge staff can also encourage participation in Refuge programs by expanding the number and types of program and special event offerings.

- The Refuge would have to take an active management role to realize these benefits. To achieve maximum results from a vehicle purchase, Refuge staff should expand program offerings, promote the use of the transit vehicle for all feasible programs and special events, and work closely with partners to maximize the use of the vehicle for partner-led programs and events.
- A transit vehicle would expand opportunities for the Refuge and its partners to offer environmental education programs to underserved communities, such as Boys and Girls Clubs, schools and assisted living centers from low-income areas, and persons with disabilities. The Refuge may want to consider making the transit vehicle available for underserved communities' group programs during times of inactivity.

APPENDIX A – CALENDAR OF TRANSIT VEHICLE ACTIVITIES

Guide to Activities Types

Blue: Refuge-led special events

Purple: Mass Audubon programs (regularly-scheduled public programs)

Green: Refuge-led Programs

Yellow: Field trips (potential future vehicle use)

Orange: Partner-led special events (potential future vehicle use)

January 2011

	Sunday	Monday	Tuesday	Wednesday	Thursday	Friday	Saturday
12/26 - 31	Dec 26	27	28	29	30	31	Jan 1, 11 9:00am 12:00pm Saturday Morning Birding
1/2 - 7	2	3	4	5 9:00am 1:00pm Audubon Wednesday Morning Birding	6	7	8 9:00am 12:00pm Saturday Morning Birding 1:00pm 4:00pm Public Interpretive Program
1/9 - 14	9	10	11 8:00am 5:00pm Hold for Group Field Trip	12 9:00am 1:00pm Audubon Wednesday Morning Birding 3:00pm 5:00pm GOMI/NHS Educatio	13 9:00am 4:00pm Volunteer/Staff Development Field Trip	14	15 9:00am 12:00pm Saturday Morning Birding
1/16 - 21	16	17	18	19 9:00am 1:00pm Audubon Wednesday Morning Birding	20	21 8:00am 5:00pm Hold for Group Field Trip	22 9:00am 4:00pm Master Naturalist Program 9:00am 12:00pm Saturday Morning Birding
1/23 - 28	23	24	25	26 9:00am 1:00pm Audubon Wednesday Morning Birding	27	28	29 9:00am 12:00pm Saturday Morning Birding
1/30 - 2/4	30	31	Feb 1	2	3	4	5

February 2011

	S	M	T	W	T	F	S
February 2011		7	1	2	3	4	5
	6	7	8	9	10	11	12
	13	14	15	16	17	18	19
	20	21	22	23	24	25	26
	27	28					

	S	M	T	W	T	F	S
March 2011			1	2	3	4	5
	6	7	8	9	10	11	12
	13	14	15	16	17	18	19
	20	21	22	23	24	25	26
	27	28	29	30	31		

	Sunday	Monday	Tuesday	Wednesday	Thursday	Friday	Saturday
Jan 30 - Feb 5	Jan 30	31	Feb 1	2 — 9:00am 1:00pm Audubon Wednesday Morning Birding	3	4	5 — 9:00am 12:00pm Saturday Morning Birding; 1:00pm 4:00pm Public Interpretive Program
Feb 6 - 12	6	7	8 — 8:00am 5:00pm Hold for Group Field Trip	9 — 9:00am 1:00pm Audubon Wednesday Morning Birding	10	11	12 — 8:00am 5:00pm Eagle Festival
Feb 13 - 19	13	14	15	16 — 9:00am 1:00pm Audubon Wednesday Morning Birding; 3:00pm 5:00pm GOMI/NHS Education Project Fie	17 — 9:00am 4:00pm Volunteer/Staff Development Field Trip	18 — 8:00am 5:00pm Hold for Group Field Trip	19 — 9:00am 4:00pm Nature Photography Workshop; 9:00am 12:00pm Saturday Morning Birding
Feb 20 - 26	20	21	22	23 — 9:00am 1:00pm Audubon Wednesday Morning Birding	24	25	26 — 9:00am 4:00pm Master Naturalist Program; 9:00am 12:00pm Saturday Morning Birding
Feb 27 - Mar 5	27 — 1:00pm 4:00pm Snowy Owl	28	Mar 1	2	3	4	5

March 2011

Sunday	Monday	Tuesday	Wednesday	Thursday	Friday	Saturday
Feb 27	**28**	**Mar 1**	**2** 9:00am 1:00pm Audubon Wednesday Morning Birding	**3**	**4**	**5** 9:00am 12:00pm Saturday Morning Birding; 1:00pm 4:00pm Public Interpretive Program
6	**7**	**8** 8:00am 5:00pm Hold for Group Field Trip	**9** 9:00am 1:00pm Audubon Wednesday Morning Birding	**10**	**11**	**12** 9:00am 12:00pm Saturday Morning Birding
13	**14**	**15**	**16** 9:00am 1:00pm Audubon Wednesday Morning Birding; 3:00pm 5:00pm GOMI/NHS Education Project Fie	**17** 9:00am 4:00pm Volunteer/Staff Development Field Trip	**18** 8:00am 5:00pm Hold for Group Field Trip	**19** 9:00am 4:00pm Master Naturalist Program; 9:00am 12:00pm Saturday Morning Birding
20	**21**	**22**	**23** 9:00am 1:00pm Audubon Wednesday Morning Birding	**24**	**25**	**26** 9:00am 12:00pm Saturday Morning Birding
27	**28**	**29**	**30** 9:00am 1:00pm Audubon Wednesday Morning Birding	**31**	**Apr 1**	**2**

Feb 27 - Mar 5
Mar 6 - 12
Mar 13 - 19
Mar 20 - 26
Mar 27 - Apr 2

April 2011

	April 2011	May 2011
	S M T W T F S 3 4 5 6 7 1 2 10 11 12 13 14 8 9 17 18 19 20 21 15 16 24 25 26 27 28 22 23 29 30	S M T W T F S 1 2 3 4 5 6 7 8 9 10 11 12 13 14 15 16 17 18 19 20 21 22 23 24 25 26 27 28 29 30 31

	Sunday	Monday	Tuesday	Wednesday	Thursday	Friday	Saturday
Mar 27 – Apr 2	Mar 27	28	29	30	31	Apr 1	2 9:00am 12:00pm Saturday Morning Birding 1:00pm 4:00pm Public Interpretive Program
Apr 3 – 9	3	4	5	6 9:00am 1:00pm Audubon Wednesday Morning Birding	7	8	9 9:00am 12:00pm Saturday Morning Birding
Apr 10 – 16	10	11	12 8:00am 5:00pm Hold for Group Field Trip	13 9:00am 1:00pm Audubon Wednesday Morning Birding 3:00pm 5:00pm GOMI/NHS Education Project Fie	14 9:00am 4:00pm Volunteer/Staff Development Field Trip	15	16 9:00am 12:00pm Saturday Morning Birding 1:00pm 4:00pm Public Interpretive Program
Apr 17 – 23	17	18	19	20 9:00am 1:00pm Audubon Wednesday Morning Birding	21	22	23 9:00am 4:00pm Master Naturalist Program 9:00am 12:00pm Saturday Morning Birding
Apr 24 – 30	24	25	26	27 9:00am 1:00pm Audubon Wednesday Morning Birding 5:00pm 8:00pm Wednesday Evening Birding	28	29 8:00am 5:00pm Hold for Group Field Trip	30 9:00am 12:00pm Saturday Morning Birding

4

May 2011

May 2011
S	M	T	W	T	F	S
1	2	3	4	5	6	7
8	9	10	11	12	13	14
15	16	17	18	19	20	21
22	23	24	25	26	27	28
29	30	31				

June 2011
S	M	T	W	T	F	S
			1	2	3	4
5	6	7	8	9	10	11
12	13	14	15	16	17	18
19	20	21	22	23	24	25
26	27	28	29	30		

Sunday	Monday	Tuesday	Wednesday	Thursday	Friday	Saturday
May 1	2	3	4 9:00am 1:00pm Audubon Wednesday Morning 5:00pm 8:00pm Wednesday Evening Birding	5	6 7:30am 11:30am Friday Morning Birding	7 9:00am 12:00pm Saturday Morning Birding 1:00pm 4:00pm Public Interpretive Program
8	9	10 8:00am 5:00pm Hold for Group Field Trip	11 9:00am 1:00pm Audubon Wednesday Morning 5:00pm 8:00pm Wednesday Evening Birding	12	13 7:30am 11:30am Friday Morning Birding	14 9:00am 12:00pm Saturday Morning Birding 1:00pm 4:00pm Public Interpretive Program
15	16	17	18 9:00am 1:00pm Audubon Wednesda 3:00pm 5:00pm GOMI/NHS Educatio 5:00pm 8:00pm Wednesday Evening	19 9:00am 4:00pm Volunteer/Staff Development Field Trip	20 7:30am 11:30am Friday Morning Birding 8:00am 5:00pm Hold for Group Field Trip	21 9:00am 4:00pm Master Naturalist Program 9:00am 12:00pm Saturday Morning Birding
22 9:00am 4:00pm Beach Clean Up Day	23	24	25 9:00am 1:00pm Audubon Wednesday Morning 5:00pm 8:00pm Wednesday Evening Birding	26	27 7:30am 11:30am Friday Morning Birding	28 9:00am 12:00pm Saturday Morning Birding
29	30	31	Jun 1	2	3	4

June 2011

Sunday	Monday	Tuesday	Wednesday	Thursday	Friday	Saturday
May 29	30	31	**Jun 1** 9:00am 1:00pm Audubon Wednesday Morning 5:00pm 8:00pm Wednesday Evening Birding	2	3	4 9:00am 12:00pm Saturday Morning Birding 1:00pm 4:00pm Public Interpretive Program
5	6	7	8 9:00am 1:00pm Audubon Wednesday Morning 5:00pm 8:00pm Wednesday Evening Birding	9	10 8:00am 5:00pm Hold for Group Field Trip	11 9:00am 4:00pm Go Fish 9:00am 12:00pm Saturday Morning Birding 1:00pm 4:00pm Public Interpretive Program
12	13	14	15 9:00am 1:00pm Audubon Wednesday Morning 3:00pm 5:00pm GOMI/NHS Education Project Fie	16 9:00am 4:00pm Volunteer/Staff Development Field Trip	17	18 9:00am 12:00pm Saturday Morning Birding 1:00pm 4:00pm Public Interpretive Program
19 9:00am 4:00pm Open House at Great Bay	20 8:00am 5:00pm Nature Photography Camp	21 8:00am 5:00pm Nature Photography Camp	22 8:00am 5:00pm Nature Photography Camp 9:00am 1:00pm Audubon Wednesday Morning Birding	23 8:00am 5:00pm Nature Photography Camp	24 8:00am 5:00pm Nature Photography Camp	25 9:00am 4:00pm Master Naturalist Program 9:00am 12:00pm Saturday Morning Birding
26	27	28 8:00am 5:00pm Hold for Group Field Trip	29 9:00am 1:00pm Audubon Wednesday Morning Birding	30	Jul 1	2

Week labels: May 29 - Jun 4 · Jun 5 - 11 · Jun 12 - 18 · Jun 19 - 25 · Jun 26 - Jul 2

June 2011
S	M	T	W	T	F	S
			1	2	3	4
5	6	7	8	9	10	11
12	13	14	15	16	17	18
19	20	21	22	23	24	25
26	27	28	29	30		

July 2011
S	M	T	W	T	F	S
					1	2
3	4	5	6	7	8	9
10	11	12	13	14	15	16
17	18	19	20	21	22	23
24	25	26	27	28	29	30
31						

July 2011

July 2011

S	M	T	W	T	F	S
3	4	5	6	7	1	2
10	11	12	13	14	8	9
17	18	19	20	21	15	16
24	25	26	27	28	22	23
31					29	30

August 2011

S	M	T	W	T	F	S
7	1	2	3	4	5	6
14	8	9	10	11	12	13
21	15	16	17	18	19	20
28	22	23	24	25	26	27
	29	30	31			

	Sunday	Monday	Tuesday	Wednesday	Thursday	Friday	Saturday
Jun 26 – Jul 2	Jun 26	27	28	29	30	Jul 1	2 — 1:00pm 4:00pm Public Interpretive Program
Jul 3 – 9	3	4	5	6 — 9:00am 1:00pm Audubon Wednesday Morning Birding	7	8 — 1:00pm 4:00pm Riverfront Music Festival	9 — 1:00pm 4:00pm Public Interpretive Program; 1:00pm 4:00pm Riverfront Music Festival
Jul 10 – 16	10	11	12 — 8:00am 5:00pm Hold for Group Field Trip	13 — 9:00am 1:00pm Audubon Wednesday Morning Birding	14 — 9:00am 4:00pm Volunteer/Staff Development Field Trip	15	16 — 1:00pm 4:00pm Public Interpretive Program
Jul 17 – 23	17	18 — 8:00am 5:00pm Parker River Refuge Academy	19 — 8:00am 5:00pm Parker River Refuge Academy	20 — 8:00am 5:00pm Parker River Refuge Academy; 9:00am 1:00pm Audubon Wednesda	21 — 8:00am 5:00pm Parker River Refuge Academy	22 — 8:00am 5:00pm Parker River Refuge Academy	23 — 9:00am 4:00pm Master Naturalist Program
Jul 24 – 30	24	25	26	27 — 9:00am 1:00pm Audubon Wednesday Morning Birding	28	29 — 8:00am 5:00pm Hold for Group Field Trip	30
Jul 31 – Aug 6	31 — 9:00am 4:00pm Yankee Homecoming	Aug 1	2	3	4	5	6

August 2011

August 2011

S	M	T	W	T	F	S
7	1	2	3	4	5	6
14	8	9	10	11	12	13
21	15	16	17	18	19	20
28	22	23	24	25	26	27
	29	30	31			

September 2011

S	M	T	W	T	F	S
				1	2	3
4	5	6	7	8	9	10
11	12	13	14	15	16	17
18	19	20	21	22	23	24
25	26	27	28	29	30	

	Sunday	Monday	Tuesday	Wednesday	Thursday	Friday	Saturday
Jul 31 – Aug 6	**Jul 31** 9:00am 4:00pm Yankee Homecoming	**Aug 1** 9:00am 4:00pm Yankee Homecoming	**2** 9:00am 4:00pm Yankee Homecoming	**3** 9:00am 4:00pm Yankee Homecoming 9:00am 1:00pm Audubon Wednesda 5:00pm 8:00pm Wednesday Evening	**4** 9:00am 4:00pm Yankee Homecoming	**5** 9:00am 4:00pm Yankee Homecoming	**6** 9:00am 12:00pm Saturday Morning Bi 1:00pm 4:00pm Public Interpretive Program
Aug 7 – 13	**7** 9:00am 4:00pm Yankee Homecoming	**8**	**9** 8:00am 5:00pm Hold for Group Field Trip	**10** 9:00am 1:00pm Audubon Wednesday Morning 5:00pm 8:00pm Wednesday Evening Birding	**11**	**12**	**13** 9:00am 12:00pm Saturday Morning Birding 1:00pm 4:00pm Public Interpretive Program
Aug 14 – 20	**14**	**15**	**16**	**17** 9:00am 1:00pm Audubon Wednesday Morning 5:00pm 8:00pm Wednesday Evening Birding	**18** 9:00am 4:00pm Volunteer/Staff Development Field Trip	**19** 8:00am 5:00pm Hold for Group Field Trip	**20** 9:00am 4:00pm Master Naturalist Program 9:00am 12:00pm Saturday Morning Bi 1:00pm 4:00pm Public Interpretive Program
Aug 21 – 27	**21**	**22**	**23**	**24** 9:00am 1:00pm Audubon Wednesday Morning 5:00pm 8:00pm Wednesday Evening Birding	**25**	**26**	**27** 9:00am 12:00pm Saturday Morning Birding
Aug 28 – Sep 3	**28**	**29**	**30**	**31** 9:00am 1:00pm Audubon Wednesday Morning 5:00pm 8:00pm Wednesday Evening Birding	**Sep 1**	**2**	**3**

September 2011

September 2011

S	M	T	W	T	F	S
4	5	6	7	1	2	3
11	12	13	14	8	9	10
18	19	20	21	15	16	17
25	26	27	28	22	23	24
				29	30	

October 2011

S	M	T	W	T	F	S
2	3	4	5	6	7	1
9	10	11	12	13	14	8
16	17	18	19	20	21	15
23	24	25	26	27	28	22
30	31					29

	Sunday	Monday	Tuesday	Wednesday	Thursday	Friday	Saturday
Aug 28 - Sep 3	Aug 28	29	30	31	Sep 1	2	**3** 9:00am 12:00pm Saturday Morning Birding; 1:00pm 4:00pm Public Interpretive Program
Sep 4 - 10	**4** 9:00am 5:00pm Buskers Festival	**5** 9:00am 5:00pm Buskers Festival	6	**7** 9:00am 1:00pm Audubon Wednesday Morning Birding	8	9	**10** 9:00am 12:00pm Saturday Morning Birding; 1:00pm 4:00pm Public Interpretive Program
Sep 11 - 17	11	12	**13** 8:00am 5:00pm Hold for Group Field Trip	**14** 9:00am 1:00pm Audubon Wednesday Morning Birding; 3:00pm 5:00pm GOMI/NHS Education Project Fie	**15** 9:00am 4:00pm Volunteer/Staff Development Field Trip	16	**17** 9:00am 4:00pm Beach Clean Up Day; 9:00am 4:00pm Trails & Sails; 9:00am 12:00pm Satur 1:00pm 4:00pm Public I
Sep 18 - 24	**18** 9:00am 4:00pm Open House at Great Bay NWR; 9:00am 4:00pm Trails & Sails	19	20	**21** 9:00am 1:00pm Audubon Wednesday Morning Birding	22	**23** 8:00am 5:00pm Hold for Group Field Trip	**24** 9:00am 4:00pm Master Naturalist Program; 9:00am 12:00pm Saturday Morning Bi; 9:00am 4:00pm Trails & Sails
Sep 25 - Oct 1	**25** 9:00am 4:00pm Trails & Sails	26	27	**28** 9:00am 1:00pm Audubon Wednesday Morning Birding	29	30	Oct 1

9

October 2011

October 2011
S	M	T	W	T	F	S
2	3	4	5	6	7	1
9	10	11	12	13	14	8
16	17	18	19	20	21	15
23	24	25	26	27	28	22
30	31					29

November 2011
S	M	T	W	T	F	S
		1	2	3	4	5
6	7	8	9	10	11	12
13	14	15	16	17	18	19
20	21	22	23	24	25	26
27	28	29	30			

	Sunday	Monday	Tuesday	Wednesday	Thursday	Friday	Saturday
9/25 - 30	Sep 25	26	27	28	29	30	Oct 1 — 9:00am 12:00pm Saturday Morning Birding; 1:00pm 4:00pm Public Interpretive Program
10/2 - 7	2	3	4	5 — 9:00am 1:00pm Audubon Wednesday Morning Birding	6	7	8 — 9:00am 12:00pm Saturday Morning Birding; 1:00pm 4:00pm Public Interpretive Program
10/9 - 14	9	10	11 — 8:00am 5:00pm Hold for Group Field Trip	12 — 9:00am 1:00pm Audubon Wednesday Morning Birding; 3:00pm 5:00pm GOMI/NHS Educatio	13 — 9:00am 4:00pm Volunteer/Staff Development Field Trip	14	15 — 9:00am 4:00pm Wildlife Day; 9:00am 12:00pm Saturday Morning Birding
10/16 - 21	16	17	18	19 — 9:00am 1:00pm Audubon Wednesday Morning Birding	20	21	22 — 9:00am 4:00pm Master Naturalist Program; 9:00am 12:00pm Saturday Morning Birding
10/23 - 28	23	24	25	26 — 9:00am 1:00pm Audubon Wednesday Morning Birding	27	28 — 8:00am 5:00pm Hold for Group Field Trip	29 — 9:00am 12:00pm Saturday Morning Birding
10/30 - 11/4	30	31	Nov 1	2	3	4	5

10

November 2011

November 2011						
S	M	T	W	T	F	S
		1	2	3	4	5
6	7	8	9	10	11	12
13	14	15	16	17	18	19
20	21	22	23	24	25	26
27	28	29	30			

December 2011						
S	M	T	W	T	F	S
				1	2	3
4	5	6	7	8	9	10
11	12	13	14	15	16	17
18	19	20	21	22	23	24
25	26	27	28	29	30	31

	Sunday	Monday	Tuesday	Wednesday	Thursday	Friday	Saturday
Oct 30 – Nov 5	Oct 30	31	Nov 1	2 — 9:00am 1:00pm Audubon Wednesday Morning Birding	3	4	5 — 9:00am 12:00pm Saturday Morning Birding; 1:00pm 4:00pm Public Interpretive Program
Nov 6 – 12	6	7	8 — 8:00am 5:00pm Hold for Group Field Trip	9 — 9:00am 1:00pm Audubon Wednesday Morning Birding	10	11	12 — 9:00am 12:00pm Saturday Morning Birding
Nov 13 – 19	13	14	15	16 — 9:00am 1:00pm Audubon Wednesday Morning Birding; 3:00pm 5:00pm GOMI/NHS Education Project Fie	17 — 9:00am 4:00pm Volunteer/Staff Development Field Trip	18 — 8:00am 5:00pm Hold for Group Field Trip	19 — 9:00am 4:00pm Master Naturalist Program; 9:00am 12:00pm Saturday Morning Birding
Nov 20 – 26	20	21	22	23 — 9:00am 1:00pm Audubon Wednesday Morning Birding	24	25	26 — 9:00am 12:00pm Saturday Morning Birding
Nov 27 – Dec 3	27	28	29	30 — 9:00am 1:00pm Audubon Wednesday Morning Birding	Dec 1	2	3

December 2011

December 2011

S	M	T	W	T	F	S
				1	2	3
4	5	6	7	8	9	10
11	12	13	14	15	16	17
18	19	20	21	22	23	24
25	26	27	28	29	30	31

January 2012

S	M	T	W	T	F	S
1	2	3	4	5	6	7
8	9	10	11	12	13	14
15	16	17	18	19	20	21
22	23	24	25	26	27	28
29	30	31				

	Sunday	Monday	Tuesday	Wednesday	Thursday	Friday	Saturday
Nov 27 – Dec 3	Nov 27	28	29 8:00am 5:00pm Hold for Group Field Trip	30	Dec 1	2	3 9:00am 12:00pm Saturday Morning Birding 1:00pm 4:00pm Public Interpretive Program
Dec 4 – 10	4	5	6	7 9:00am 1:00pm Audubon Wednesday Morning Birding	8	9	10 9:00am 12:00pm Saturday Morning Birding
Dec 11 – 17	11	12	13	14 9:00am 1:00pm Audubon Wednesday Morning Birding 3:00pm 5:00pm GOMI/NHS Education Project Fie	15 9:00am 4:00pm Volunteer/Staff Development Field Trip	16 8:00am 5:00pm Hold for Group Field Trip	17 9:00am 4:00pm Master Naturalist Program 9:00am 12:00pm Saturday Morning Birding
Dec 18 – 24	18	19	20	21 9:00am 1:00pm Audubon Wednesday Morning Birding	22	23	24 9:00am 12:00pm Saturday Morning Birding
Dec 25 – 31	25	26	27	28 9:00am 1:00pm Audubon Wednesday Morning Birding	29	30	31 9:00am 12:00pm Saturday Morning Birding

APPENDIX B – SHUTTLING OPTION

Shuttle Option Description

When the transit vehicle is not being utilized for scheduled activities, the Refuge may consider offering a special program to serve regional transit users across the Boston metropolitan area. The shuttle option would pick up visitors at the Newburyport MBTA commuter rail station, stop at the Refuge Headquarters, drive passengers through the Refuge as part of a guided tour, deposit passengers in downtown Newburyport for free time to spend in shops and restaurants, and transfer passengers back to the rail station. The shuttle option would allow more visitors to access the Refuge during high visitation periods within a structured program led by Refuge staff so as not to increase negative impacts to refuge resources. It would also allow individuals without private vehicles to visit the Refuge via public transportation and provide ancillary economic development benefits to the City of Newburyport by introducing new visitors to the downtown commercial area. The neighboring Town of Ipswich has collaborated with their local transit authority to provide a similar service to Crane Beach (see side box).

In order for such a program to be successful, Refuge staff would have to schedule the program around the MBTA schedule and work with partners (including the MBTA, the City of Newburyport, and the Newburyport Chamber of Commerce) to promote the program both locally and throughout the region. The Refuge would be able to leverage such programs and the amenities of Newburyport to expand visitor opportunities, while the City of Newburyport would benefit from an additional transportation option for visitors arriving by train to Newburyport. Both entities should work collaboratively to best market and leverage such events, including aligning schedules and services with potential local activities.

The shuttle option should include collaboration with the MBTA for marketing and ticket purchasing. The Refuge and MBTA could jointly offer a streamlined ticket purchasing option that includes the cost of the commuter rail fare and a program fee for the Refuge shuttle and tour. The MBTA can also promote the Refuge programs among its riders in the metropolitan Boston area. Such a partnership may assist in growing a program and increasing awareness which would in turn increase visitation to both the Refuge and the city of Newburyport.

Shuttle Option Schedules

The following shuttle option routes and timetables align with transit vehicle availability (see Appendix A) and the MBTA commuter rail schedule.[69]

> ### *Ipswich Essex Explorer Shuttle*
>
> The Cape Ann Transportation Authority (CATA) offers transit service on Cape Ann, approximately 30 miles south of the Refuge. CATA operates a seasonal shuttle that connects the MBTA commuter rail with area attractions. The Ipswich Essex Explorer offers service to Crane Beach, Wolf Hollow, the Essex Shipbuilding Museum, and area shops and restaurants. Operating on summer weekends and holidays only, the shuttle collects passengers up to seven times per day at the Ipswich rail station (coinciding with trail arrivals), and offers up to seven return trips from featured destinations to the train station.
>
> One-way fares are $1.50 for adults and children 5 and over, or passengers can purchase a $5 Beach Pass, which includes round-trip bus fare and the entrance fee for Crane Beach. The Town of Ipswich contributes funds for the operation of the Explorer service.

---

[69] Massachusetts Bay Transportation Authority. 2011. Newburyport/Rockport Line Schedules and Maps. Accessed 18 May 2011: http://www.mbta.com/schedules_and_maps/rail/lines/?route=NBRYROCK

Weekend Option

The Refuge and its partners have relatively few activities scheduled in Sundays, as evidenced in Appendix A. Therefore, the shuttle option is scheduled around the Sunday MBTA commuter rail timetable. The Refuge may consider running the shuttle option on Saturdays as well, based on the availability of the transit vehicle. Shuttle option programs on Sundays could include a mid-day event (shorter duration) or an afternoon event (longer duration) and would follow the following schedule for visitors arriving from the Newburyport/Rockport line of the MBTA commuter rail (with service to Boston's North Station).

Mid-day Sunday Events
- Northbound train departs Boston at 9:30 AM and arrives in Newburyport at 10:30 AM
- Refuge shuttle pickup at MBTA Station (arrive at 10:30 AM and depart at 10:45 AM)
- Transportation to the Refuge HQ, arriving at 11:00 AM
- Tour of Refuge from 11:00 AM to 1:00 PM
- Depart from the Refuge at 1:00 PM with service to downtown Newburyport (arrive downtown at 1:15 PM).
- Free time in Newburyport from 1:15-2:25 PM, with a shuttle departing the city center at 2:25 PM with service to the MBTA commuter rail station.
- Southbound train departs from Newburyport at 2:48 pm and arrives in Boston at 3:49 PM

Afternoon Sunday Events
- Northbound train departs Boston at 11:30 AM and arrives in Newburyport at 12:30 PM
- Refuge shuttle pickup at MBTA Station (arrive at 12:30 PM and depart at 12:45 PM)
- Transportation to the Refuge HQ, arriving at 1:00 PM
- Tour of Refuge from 1:00 PM to 3:00 PM
- Depart from the Refuge at 3:00 PM with service to downtown Newburyport (arrive downtown at 3:15 PM)
- Free time in Newburyport from 3:15-5:25 PM, with a shuttle departing the city center at 5:25 PM with service to the MBTA commuter rail station
- Southbound train departs from Newburyport at 5:48 PM and arrives in Boston at 6:49 PM

The afternoon schedule would permit an extra hour of visitation in downtown Newburyport.

Weekday Option

Several weekday options may exist depending on the Refuge's calendar of events and staff or resource availability. Mondays, Tuesdays, and Fridays have the greatest availability for a shuttle vehicle. The MBTA schedule is consistent for all weekdays, so the schedule listed below could be used on any weekday. To allow flexibility for visitors to spend more time in Newburyport, the Refuge could run two shuttles to the MBTA station.

Weekday Events
- Northbound train departs Boston at 9:45 AM and arrives in Newburyport at 10:46 AM
- Refuge shuttle pickup at MBTA Station (arrive at 10:45 AM and depart at 11:00 AM)
- Transportation to the Refuge HQ, arriving at 11:15 AM

- Tour of Refuge from 11:15 AM to 1:15 PM
- Depart from the Refuge at 1:15 PM with service to downtown Newburyport (arrive downtown at 1:30 PM)
- *OPTION 1:*
  - Free time in Newburyport from 1:30 to 2:30 PM, with a shuttle departing the city center at 2:30 PM with service to the MBTA commuter rail station
  - Southbound trains departs from Newburyport at 2:48 PM and arrives in Boston at 3:52 PM
- *OPTION 2:*
  - Free time in Newburyport from 1:30 to 4:10 PM, with a shuttle departing the city center at 4:10 PM with service to the MBTA commuter rail station
  - Southbound trains departs from Newburyport at 4:35 PM and arrives in Boston at 5:41 PM

Shuttle Pilot

The Refuge should test the shuttle option on a pilot basis to assess demand and feasibility. The project team recommends an initial pilot of a Sunday shuttle option once a month from May to October, with potential to expand to a weekly Sunday shuttle and a weekly Tuesday or Friday shuttle. The provision of a shuttle service held one day per week for the peak visitation season (May through October) would result in roughly 715 additional miles traveled by the transit vehicle per year; one weekday and one weekend service option during peak visitation season would result in 1,430 additional miles per year.

Refuge staff should consider the following as part of a pilot program:

1. *Reservations and Demand:* Visitors would need to reserve seats in advance, due to limited capacity in a 28-passenger transit vehicle. Refuge staff or volunteers could manage a reservation system, which may include an online form or a call-in option. The Refuge staff should track the number of people who sign up for the shuttle, including those that cannot be accommodated due to limited capacity.
2. *Fares and Fees:* The Refuge would need to collect a small fee to cover the cost of vehicle use. This could ideally be purchased in combination with an MBTA commuter rail fare. The Refuge should calculate the fee based on fuel cost, staff time, Refuge entry fee, and a general vehicle use fee. An initial fee assessment for educational and interpretive programs, as calculated in Section 6, suggested that the Refuge may elect to charge $3 for adults and $1 for children. The Refuge may also consider charging an additional one to three dollars per person for a shuttle service or request funds from the City of Newburyport. The Refuge may consider discounted fees for seniors, children, and/or families. Refuge staff may also informally discuss appropriate fees with shuttle participants or test multiple fee structures during the pilot.
3. *Loading and Parking in Newburyport:* Refuge would need to coordinate with the City of Newburyport to identify appropriate loading and parking areas downtown. The City may also provide maps or other promotional materials to shuttle visitors, including maps of the Clipper City Rail Trail for pedestrian access to the MBTA station.
4. *Visitor Use Data:* The Refuge should collect the following types of data about participants: origin, method of transport from origin (commuter rail or private vehicle to commuter rail lot), age category (senior, adult, or child), and mobility level. The Refuge should also record the total number of participants for each shuttle option event, including participants that tried to make a reservation but could not be accommodated.

www.ingramcontent.com/pod-product-compliance
Lightning Source LLC
Chambersburg PA
CBHW080424290526
45791CB00008BA/2395